GORGEOUS GEORGIANS

TWO HORRIBLE

HORRIBLE HISTORIES

BOOKS IN ONE

VILE VICTORIANS

WITHDRAWN

TERRY DEARY ILLUSTRATED BY **MARTIN BROWN**

SCHOLASTIC

Scholastic Children's Books
Euston House, 24 Eversholt Street,
London, NW1 1DB, UK

A division of Scholastic Ltd
London ~ New York ~ Toronto ~ Sydney ~ Auckland
Mexico City ~ New Delhi ~ Hong Kong

First published in this edition by Scholastic Ltd, 1999
This edition published 2009

The Gorgeous Georgians
First published in the UK by Scholastic Ltd, 1998
Text copyright © Terry Deary, 1998
Illustrations copyright © Martin Brown, 1998

The Vile Victorians
First published in the UK by Scholastic Ltd, 1994
Text copyright © Terry Deary, 1994
Illustrations copyright © Martin Brown, 1994

All rights reserved

ISBN 978 1407 10967 1

Page layout services provided by Quadrum Solutions Ltd, Mumbai, India
Printed and bound in the UK by CPI Bookmarque, Croydon, Surrey

10 9 8 7 6 5 4 3 2 1

CONTENTS

Gorgeous Georgians

Introduction 7

Timeline 9

Gorgeous Georgians 12

Gorging Georgians 22

Top of the class 30

Gruesome Georgians 53

Bodies for sale 68

Quaint quack doctors 78

Gory Georgian fun and games 86

Wacky Georgian words 99

Rotten revolutions 102

Test your teacher 120

Epilogue 127

Grisly Quiz 131

Interesting Index 139

CONTENTS

Vile Victorians

Introduction 145

Vile Victorians timelines 147

Vile Victorian Queen 152

Vile Victorian childhood 162

Vile Victorian schools 184

Vile Victorian fun and games 194

Vile Victorian poems, plays and songs 204

Vile Victorian life 213

Vile Victorian food 230

Vile Victorian facts 234

The vile Victorian Army 239

Vile Victorian villains 252

Epilogue 268

Grisly Quiz 269

Interesting Index 277

GORGEOUS GEORGIANS

Timeline

1714 Queen Anne of the Stuart family dies. George I comes from Hanover (Germany) to take the English throne. He's not popular, but the other Stuarts are Catholics and most Brits don't want that.

1715 Stuart supporters want James III to rule so they have a rebellion in support of him – these 'Jacobite' rebellions are crushed … for now.

1727 George II comes to the throne when George I has a violent attack of diarrhoea and dies. Pooh!

1745 Bonnie Prince Charlie – the last of the Stuart family – lands in Scotland to claim the throne of Britain in another Jacobite rebellion. The Scottish clans are brutally beaten by the Brit Army.

1750 First organized police force in London – the Bow Street Runners.

1760 George III comes to the throne – and stays for 60 years in sickness and in health.

1770 Captain Cook claims Australia for Britain. He doesn't bother to ask the Aborigines if they want to be British, of course.

1775 American colonies rebel against British rule.

1788 Australia welcomes its first

9

British convicts. It's a good place to dump them. And only 48 die on the voyage!

1789 The French peasants revolt against their rulers. Soon they'll be slicing noble heads off with the guillotine.

1792 First gas lighting in houses, invented by some bright spark.

1793 The French have chopped their King Louis' head. Now they're looking for a fight and pick on Britain. The start of 20 years of wars – the Napoleonic Wars.

1798 Steam-powered spinning mill opens in Bradford. Bad news for spinners working from home, being replaced by machines. They'll all have to take jobs at the dangerous, dirty factories.

1801 Ireland joins Great Britain and another red cross is added to the flag to make the Union Jack.

1804 Captain Dick's Puffer starts running! The first steam railway locomotive, invented by Richard Trevithick.

1805 British Navy wins Battle of Trafalgar against the French and lose their admiral, Horatio, Lord Nelson, potted by a hot-shot.

1806 Steam-powered looms invented.

Bad news for weavers.

1807 Britain bans slave trading – having made a fortune out of it for the past hundred years or so.

1811 Out of work weavers wreck the machines that put them out of work. They call themselves Luddites and male wreckers often dress as women!

1815 Britain defeats Napoleon and his French armies at Waterloo. (A village in Belgium, not a London station.)

1819 It's now against the law for children under nine to work or for older children to work more than 12 hours a day.

1820 Popular (but blind, deaf and mad) George III dies. Unpopular (fat and dishonest) George IV takes over.

1825 First steam-driven passenger railway runs from Stockton to Darlington. Crowds turn up to watch … they are disappointed when it doesn't explode!

1830 Fat George IV dies and his brother, boring William IV, takes over. End of Georgian age.

1837 Queen Victoria comes to the throne. A right madam who will reign even longer than George III.

Gorgeous Georgians

Vicious verses and cruel cartoons

The Georgians could be very cruel to one another. They had their own way of mocking people.

Poets, like Alexander Pope (1688–1744) were especially nasty. (Lady Mary Wortley Montague called him 'the wicked asp of Twickenham'.) His poems poked fun at people but especially people who loved themselves.

Unimportant note 1: The posh word for cruel fun is satire – remember that word!

The other cruel artists were cartoonists. Men like Hogarth (1629-1764) – he made people look ridiculous in his drawings.

Unimportant note 2: The posh word for this is caricature – remember that word too!

Georgian makeover

By the 1770s some of the fashions became quite ridiculous. So here's a *satire* and a *caricature* of ladies' fashion in the age of George III. (And now you can forget those two words. Which two words? Er … I've forgotten.)

Modern magazines offer readers a 'makeover' – they say they'll change someone's appearance from grot to hot in ten easy steps. If the Georgians did a makeover then the results would have been just as stunning…

1. *White is beautiful, dear ladies,*
   Smear your face with paint of lead;
   Never mind the lead has made
   The men who mixed it ill … or dead.

~ Make-up is a flat white lead paint

YOU CAN DRAG A HORSE TO WATER BUT A FACE PAINT MUST BE LEAD

2. *Take some silk of red or black,*
   Cut a circle or a crescent;
   Stick it to your face to cover
   Smallpox scars … it's much more pleasant.

~Silk beauty spots are cut out and stuck on

DALMATIANS ARE VERY FASHIONABLE THIS YEAR

3. *Take some plaster, dyed bright red,*
   Crush it to a ruby paste;
   Smear it on your lips, dear ladies,
   Never mind the chalky taste.

~Red Plaster of Paris is used for lips

DON'T SMILE OR YOUR LIPS'LL DROP OFF

PLASTER

13

4. *Shave your eyebrows clean away,*
Take a trap and catch some mice;
Make false eyebrows from the mouse skin,
Stick them on to look so nice.

~ Black lead eyelashes and mouse-skin eyebrows are needed

CHEESE MADAM?

YUMMY!

YES PLEASE!

5. *Make your face look sweet and chubby,*
Pack your mouth with balls of cork;
Fit your false teeth in the middle,
Hope you don't choke when you talk.

~ Cork balls held in the cheeks improve the face

BUT MADAM, CRICKET BALLS ARE MADE OF CORK!

6. *Next you need a monster wig*
If you want to look real smashin';
When your wig has reached the ceiling
Then you'll be the height of fashion!

~ Build up the hair like a pyramid

I'M SURE MADAM'S UMBRELLA IS IN THERE SOMEWHERE

14

7. Decorate your lovely hairpiece,
Use the feathers of a parrot;
Add some ribbons, fruit and flowers,
From your ears then hang a carrot.

~Never wear your hair plain

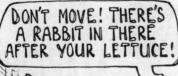

DON'T MOVE! THERE'S A RABBIT IN THERE AFTER YOUR LETTUCE!

8. Wear a dress of finest satin,
Over wide, hooped petticoats;
When you walk along the pavement
Push pedestrians in the road.

~Wide skirts and long trains are the fashion

I'M UNDER HERE!

9. Don't forget to take your handbag,
Fill it with the usual stuff;
Perfume and sweet vinegar.
To clear your head you'll need some snuff.

~Fashionable ladies clear their heads with snuff

AHSHEW!

BLESS YOU MADAM

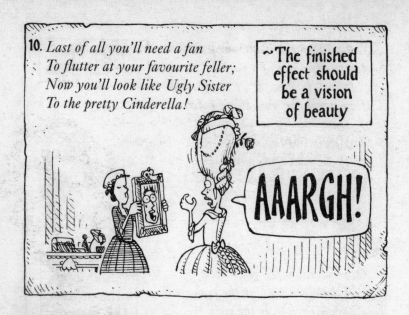

10. *Last of all you'll need a fan*
To flutter at your favourite feller;
Now you'll look like Ugly Sister
To the pretty Cinderella!

~The finished effect should be a vision of beauty

AAARGH!

Heights of fashion

It wasn't only poets and cartoonists who made fun of ladies. A theatre director called Garrick had a character on stage dressed with every kind of vegetable and a carrot dangling from each ear. Of course real ladies never wore carrots – but they did wear the scarlet flowers of runner beans!

BZZZZZZZZZZZZZZZZZZZ...

In 1786 four overdressed ladies were scoffed at as they entered the theatre. Actresses stopped the play and returned wearing similarly ridiculous dress to make fun of the ladies.

In the 1780s the high hair went out of fashion. The writer Addison said…

I remember the time when ladies' hair shot up to a great height so that women were so much taller than men. We appeared like grasshoppers beside them. I remember ladies who were once nearly seven feet high and are now a few inches short of five feet.

Fans were waved in front of the face to keep a lady cool in the steaming hot theatres. Some men complained that the large fans were more like windmills! They were decorated with pictures but also with verses of songs or paragraphs from popular books. (If you got bored at the opera you could always read your fan.) Ladies learned to use fan-fluttering as a signal to people watching. One flutter might mean anger while another flutter might mean love. Fans were also useful to hide a lady's mouth if she had rotten teeth. And they could wave away the foul smell if she had bad breath.

Dresses were worn over wide, hooped petticoats. These came into fashion in 1710 and went out of fashion in 1780 – but at the royal court they were still being worn over 40 years later. A writer complained that when one young lady walked down the street she took up the full width of the pavement.

Did you know…?

In 1776 a lady made the mistake of wearing a decorated hat in the country. It was covered in fruit and vegetables which were fastened on with metal pins. As she sat down for a picnic a passing cow rushed across to eat the hat. Sadly it ate the metal pins too. One stuck in its throat and the cow died a few hours later.

Gorgeous Georgian men

It's easy to poke fun at Georgian women but the men were just as bad. They were known as *fops*, meaning *posers* (and other ruder words!).

1 From 1660 till 1760 it was the century of the slapheads. Men wore wigs – even when they weren't bald! Wigs were popular until the 1760s. They could be very expensive so they were often stolen. Thieves would ride on the back of a carriage, carefully cut a hole through the back, snatch a wig off the passenger and jump off.

2 But wigs could be nasty, filthy things. Topham Beauclark took pleasure in shaking bugs out of his wig in front of lady friends. Many men shaved their heads so the wigs would fit. If they took the wigs off in the comfort of their own home they wore a night-cap (like Wee Willie Winkie!) to keep their heads warm. Really fashionable men wore a turban!

3 Wigs were held in place with powder (made from flour, nutmeg, starch and, maybe, gold dust). Even when wigs went out of fashion a gentleman would hold his hair in place with powder. Walking behind a gentleman on a windy day could choke you! When Prime Minister Pitt put a tax on hair powder in 1795 men stopped using it.

4 Many fops became very fussy about keeping clean and had regular baths. But the clothes of some men were as bad as the dirty wigs. Chelsea pensioners took lice from their coats and bet on races between them.

5 Umbrellas came into fashion in Stuart times but were more common in gorgeous Georgian days. But men who used umbrellas were jeered at in the street. Even in 1797 they were a rare sight – in Cambridge, there was only one umbrella in the whole town. It was kept in a shop and you could hire it if you were caught in a shower.

6 Rich gentlemen could afford clothes just as gorgeous as the ladies'. Silk or velvet coats could be embroidered with silver thread and trimmed with lace. Gorgeous! But the collars and neck-cloths that became popular in the 1820s were starched and ironed till they were stiff as a board. There were reports that some stiff collars chopped off the ear lobes of the young men who wore them!

7 The three-cornered hat, famous in pictures of highwaymen and pirates, was popular in the 1700s. But towards the end of the century an amazing new fashion appeared. Tall, silk, top hats. (You'll have seen them at weddings perhaps.) But the Georgians were amazed when they first saw them. A writer said, 'Women fainted at the sight, children screamed and dogs yelped.'

8 Fashionable young men of the early 1770s were known as Macaronis. They wore thick white make-up, cheek blusher and lipstick. George IV was especially vain about his appearance. He covered his ruddy face in chalk dust and even used leeches to suck his blood to try to make him pale. George also wore a corset to make his bulging waist thinner but his friend, Beau Brummel, told him his trousers didn't fit anyway. George burst into tears.

9 Beau Brummel himself was a leader of men's fashion in Georgian Britain. He plucked or shaved his face several times every day and used three hairdressers. He refused to wear make-up and bathed regularly … unlike many of his smelly friends. When he argued with George IV he became unpopular and died mad and penniless.

10 Men changed their shape with padding worn under their clothes. They padded the calves of their legs so they didn't look skinny when they wore tight trousers and put pads on their chests to make them look mightier than Tarzan!

I THINK I'VE GOT MY PADDING ON THE WRONG WAY

Gorging Georgians

Clever cakes

You've probably heard the rhyme:

> *Pat-a-cake, pat-a-cake baker's man!*
> *Bake me a cake as fast as you can;*
> *Pat it and prick it and mark it with 'B',*
> *Put it in the oven for Baby and me.*

But do you know what 'mark it with "B"' means? No? Ask your teacher. Surprise, surprise, they don't know either.

A Georgian child could have told your teacher that a lot of people cooked over open fires and didn't have ovens. They could roast meat or boil puddings but they couldn't *bake* a cake. So a cook would mix a cake and take it to the local baker to bake in his oven. They didn't want their cake mixed up with someone else's, so they marked it with their initial … 'B' for 'baby' in this case.

If your name was Sarah Isobel Catherine King, or Benjamin Uriah Morton, or even Philip Oliver Nigel George Young, then you wouldn't want all of your initials on the cake – would you?

And cake was eaten at breakfast as well as teatime.

COME ON NOW, EAT YOUR BREAKFAST

Clever cooks and minding manners

Here are some Georgian inventions that made life tastier.

1 Tasty toast The Georgians invented toast. A nasty Swedish visitor said the English invented toast because their houses were too chilly to spread butter on cold bread!

2 Yummy Yorkshires Ovens were improved so you could roast meat and cook a batter pudding in one at the same time. This pudding became known as a Yorkshire pudding. (Probably because it was eaten with roast Yorkshire terrier – only joking!) Yorkshire pudding was often a treat for Christmas Day.

3 Chocolate chunks Chocolate was drunk at the end of the 1600s – mixed with wine! The wine was heated and the chunk of chocolate grated into it. Sounds disgusting. Later, water was used to make hot chocolate and by the end of the 1700s you could eat chocolate bars.

4 Terrific tea Tea and coffee were also popular with the rich in Georgian times. Tea was so expensive it was kept in a tea caddy with a lock on. There was a good trade in used tea-leaves. Traders put some colour back into the old tea leaves with chemicals. These chemicals could make you ill – or even kill you – but the traders didn't mind too much. (After all, they didn't drink the stuff!)

5 Spiffing spits Some cooks still roasted meat on a spit, but a Georgian spit could be turned by a clockwork motor. Poor people still roasted meat (when they could afford it) by hanging it by a hook from the mantelpiece over the fire. This was known as a 'danglespit' – no prizes for guessing why.

6 Super sandwiches In 1760 John Montague, the fourth Earl of Sandwich, was playing cards and didn't want to stop for dinner. He ordered that his meat be slapped between two pieces of bread so he could eat it while he played. Everyone started to copy him and asked for 'A beef as-eaten-by-John-Montague-the-fourth-Earl-of-Sandwich, please.' (The Romans had this idea more than 1,000 years before, but you don't eat a jam julius caesar, a ham hadrian or a peanut butter nero. You eat a *sandwich*.)

7 Kindly cooks At the start of the Georgian age butchers used to kill their animals in some cruel ways. (You really wouldn't want to know what they did to turkeys because it would ruin Christmas for you forever.) One recipe told a cook, 'Take a red cockerel that is not too old and beat him to death.' (Battered chicken is still popular today – but it's not quite the same thing!) By the end of the Georgian period, you'll be pleased to hear, the killing of animals for food was kinder – but the animals still ended up just as dead.

8 Trendy teatime In the early 1700s people had dinner at two or three pm. By the end of the century this had moved to six or seven pm. Of course you'd get hungry long before that so fashionable people had 'afternoon tea' at about four o'clock. Did you realize that

your four o'clock tin of beans makes you a trendy Georgian?

9 Fab fruits The Georgians started to eat raw fruit. In earlier times doctors had said that eating fruit could spread

the plague! With new 'hot houses' the Georgians could grow their own exotic fruits, like grapes, peaches and pineapples. They also grew tomatoes and cooked them, but it was another 100 years before they ate them raw.

10 Cool rules Georgians wrote down rules on how the upper classes ought to behave at meal times. (You may like to try these at school dinners.)

- Guests walk in to the dining room in order, ladies first. Ladies and gentlemen sit next to one another. (At the start of the 1700s all the women had sat at one end and the men at the other.)
- Don't eat too quickly, because it shows you are too hungry.
- Don't eat too slowly, because that might mean you don't like your food.

- Never sniff your food when it's on the fork or the cook will think it's rotten.
- Don't scratch yourself, spit, blow your nose, lean your elbows on the table or sit too far back from the table.
- Do *not* pick your teeth before the plates are removed.
- If you need to go to the toilet then go and return quietly without telling everyone where you're going. (This was a great improvement on earlier dinner arrangements where pots were kept in the dining room for people to pee in!)

Did you know…?
Over in the American colonies in 1748 a schoolboy copied out rules from a French book of manners. He wrote, 'Do not clean your teeth with your fork, your knife or the tablecloth.' Clean your teeth with a tablecloth? Sadly the boy who wrote that mustn't have cleaned his teeth with *anything* because he ended up with false teeth made of wood. The boy's name was George Washington and he grew up to be America's first president.

Fatten up your friends

William Verral wrote a book called *The Cook's Paradise* with recipes for cooks to try. You can invite your friends to try this fairly simple recipe and it's pretty certain that it won't kill them. They may even enjoy it and invite you to share their next school dinner with you.

Strawberry fritters

You need:

450 g large strawberries (More if you have a lot of friends)

175 g plain flour

50 g caster sugar

2 teaspoons grated nutmeg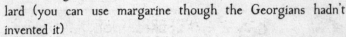

2 eggs

225 ml single cream

lard (you can use margarine though the Georgians hadn't invented it)

Method: Start this at least two hours before your guests arrive.

1 Dry the strawberries but leave the stalks on so you can hold them when you eat them.

2 Mix the flour, nutmeg and sugar in a bowl.

3 Beat the eggs, stir in the cream and slowly stir the mixture into the flour and sugar.

4 Leave this batter to stand for two hours.

5 Heat some lard in a frying pan. (It's best to get an adult to do this. If anyone's going to get burned it may as well be an adult rather than you. Adults are also useful for washing up your mess afterwards.)

6 Dip each strawberry in the batter – holding it by the stalk.

7 Drop a few strawberries into the hot lard and fry them gently till they are golden brown.

8 Drain them on kitchen towel and keep them warm in an oven while you cook the rest.

9 Eat the strawberries but not the stalks.

10 If you like them then share them with your friends. If you absolutely adore them then scoff the lot, describe the taste to your friends ... and tell them to cook their own.

Foul food

Not everything in the Georgian pantry was as tasty as strawberry fritters. There are a few gorgeous Georgian foods you may not like so much.

1 Daniel Defoe, the author of *Robinson Crusoe*, described his visit to Stilton, the town famous for its cheese…

> *The cheese is brought to the table with the mites or maggots round it so thick that they bring a spoon with them to eat the mites with, as you do the cheese.*

2 A doctor and writer, Tobias Smollett, complained about London bread…

> *The bread I eat in London is a harmful paste mixed with chalk and bone ashes, tasteless and bad for the health. The people know what is in it but prefer it to good corn bread because it is whiter.*

IT'S TOTALLY POISONOUS BUT VERY WHITE

I'LL TAKE TWO

Smollett died when he was just 50. Maybe he ate too much bread!

3 Writer Jonathan Swift (famous for his book *Gulliver's Travels*) came up with a cure for the problem of food shortages in Ireland…

I have been told that a young, healthy child of a year old is a most delicious, nourishing and wholesome food, whether it's stewed, toasted, baked or boiled. I humbly suggest that 100,000 infants may be offered for sale to rich people in the kingdom. The mothers should try to make sure that they are plump and fat and good for the table.

I LOVE CHILDREN... BUT I COULDN'T EAT A WHOLE ONE

(He was joking, but making a serious point about how the Irish were treated.)

4 When a scientist took a close look at pepper he discovered that there was more in it than peppercorns. There was also the sweepings from the floors of the store-rooms. If there were mice and rats in the store-rooms then their droppings would be ground up with the pepper-powder. Of course, French shopkeepers ground in powdered dogs' droppings.

5 Milk was sold on the streets of cities by milk maids who carried it round the streets in open pails. The trouble was the pails collected extras on their journey. Tobias Smollett described them…

Dirty water thrown from windows, spittle, snot and tobacco squirts from passersby, spatterings from coach wheels, dirt and trash chucked into it by roguish boys for the joke's sake, the spewings of infants and finally the lice that drop from the rags of the nasty drab woman that sells this precious mixture.

Top of the class

Daniel Defoe went on a tour of Britain and described the country. He thought Manchester was the 'greatest village in England' – so he'd be pleased to know the village football team is now doing well. He wrote that Liverpool was 'one of the wonders of Britain', and this was 200 years before The Beatles!

He also saw some pretty dreadful sights, especially among the poor people. The old ways were changing and, as usual, it meant the poor got poorer and the rich got richer. One of the problems was 'Enclosure.'

'What's that?' you cry! (Or if you *don't* cry it then your teacher probably will – and expect you to write about it in your next test.) So here's N. Idiot's guide to Enclosure...

HELLO! I AM N. IDIOT. NOW, YOU CAN CALL ME AN IDIOT IF YOU LIKE...BUT THINGS WERE BETTER IN THE GOOD OLD DAYS

The GOOD old DAYS before ENCLOSURE

Peasants share Common Land and Grow Crops.

Happy Peasant with his pig.

Happy Peasant's wife spins wool in happy cottage.

Unhappy Lord in Manor House wants that common land.

Happy pig and happy sheep.

Happy Peasants happy children helping in the fields.

ENCLOSURE ACTS AFTER 1720 GOT RID OF THE OPEN FIELDS ALL OVER BRITAIN. MORE MONEY COULD BE MADE BY LESS PEOPLE

The BAD GEORGIAN days of ENCLOSURE

Fields fenced off so one Landowner can make more money.

Unhappy Peasant has to find work in town.

Unhappy Peasant's wife has to work in miserable mill.

Happy Lord in Manor House owns the lot.

TOWN

Unhappy Peasant children have to work in seedy slums, foul factories or murky mines.

Happy pig and sheep with flocks of friends.

ENCLOSURE MADE 'BRITAIN' RICHER... AND MOST OF HER PEOPLE POORER. NOW, CALL ME AN IDIOT, BUT I WONDER IF IT WAS WORTH IT?

Daniel Defoe reckoned there were *seven* classes of people in Georgian Britain. Nothing is ever that simple, of course. But here are Defoe's seven classes. Which one would you like to have been in?

Class 7: 'The miserable, who really suffer want' In 1757 a mother and nine children in Buckinghamshire went several days without food. The mother found some money and bought the heart, liver and lungs of a calf to make a meal. Then she went off to gather fire wood. When she got back the children had eaten every scrap, gullet and all.

The same year a mother and two children in Cumberland had no bread and tried to survive on horse bran. They were all found dead one morning and the children had straw in their mouths.

Class 6: 'The poor, whose lives are hard' A family of seven in Derbyshire lived in a cave. The father was a lead miner and had been born in the cave, so had his five children. The cave was divided into three rooms by curtains and a hole had been dug through the roof to make a chimney. A pig and its piglets ran round the door. The miner earned about £6 a year and his wife could wash the lead ore and earn another £4 a year. Defoe wrote…

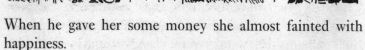

> *Things inside did not look as miserable as I'd expected. Everything was clean and neat and they seemed to live very pleasantly. The children looked plump and healthy, the woman was tall, clean and attractive.*

When he gave her some money she almost fainted with happiness.

Class 5: 'The country people, who manage indifferently' (not too well) The days of the peasant families with their own strips of land were finished in Georgian times. A writer said the main problem was the country people owned nothing. Before Enclosure they used

to keep a cow and a pony, a goose and a pig on the 'common' land. They'd have the odd wild rabbit, nuts and berries. But the common land was fenced off and sold to the richer farmers. The poor workers couldn't afford a large farm and there weren't any small ones. What was the point in working? A writer said...

Go to an ale house in the country and what will you find? It is full of men who could be working. They ask, 'If I work hard will I be allowed to build my own cottage? No. If I stay sober will I have land for a cow? No. If I save up can I get half an acre for potatoes? No. All you are offering me is the workhouse! Bring me another pot of ale.'

Life in the country wasn't fresh air and roses. You worked when the farmer wanted you – harvest or sowing times – and you went hungry the rest of the year.

Class 4: 'The working trades, who labour hard but feel no want' The workers worked long hours, in terrible conditions, for poor pay. Yet in the north of England from the 1790s, tens of thousands flocked to the mills in the towns to get away from the country. They crowded into dark, filthy houses so they could be near their work. With children as young as five working, a family would have enough to eat and stay warm, but it wasn't much of a life.

33

Spinners worked 14 hours a day in steamy temperatures up to 90°C – it had to be steamy to stop the thread snapping.

The weavers were better paid and could earn £2 to £3 a week when Defoe was writing. But within a hundred years machines were replacing them and their wages fell to 12 shillings (60p) a week.

Builders built houses in the factory towns especially for weavers. They were built over ditches so the weavers could work in a nice damp cellar. It ruined their health but at least the threads didn't snap.

Class 3: 'The middle sort, who live well' The people in the middle didn't do too badly. Priests could be poor, but some had some very good parishes and lived very comfortably. A lady went to dinner with the Rector of Aston in 1779 and described her meal…

At three o'clock we sat down at table. It was covered at one end with a salmon in fennel sauce, melted butter, lemon pickle and soy; at the other end was a loin of veal roasted, on one side kidney beans, on the other side peas and in the middle a hot pigeon pie with yolk of egg in it. Next we were offered chicken and ham, then a currant tart followed by gooseberries, currants and melon, wines and cider.

Class 2: 'The rich, who live plentifully'

Some rich people thought the local village spoiled the view from their great houses ... so they knocked the village down and moved the poor somewhere else.

But other rich Georgians made their wealth by trading in people. Slavers. They captured Africans, transported them across the Atlantic Ocean like cattle and sold the ones who survived.

The slave journey wasn't the worst part of the experience. Being a slave was miserable. Nicholas Cresswell, a visitor to the West Indies in 1774, described their life...

We went ashore and saw a cargo of slaves land. They were all naked except for a small piece of blue cloth. If they made the slightest mistake they were tied up and whipped without mercy. Some of them die under this harsh treatment.

Class 1: 'The great, who live profusely' (with a lot to spare)

Most lords managed to earn £5,000 a year – that's about £300,000 today. They enjoyed their money. Some of the great country houses you can see today were built in the Georgian period. In 1762 George III bought 'The Queen's House' in London

and turned it into Buckingham Palace. (It cost him £21,000 – the price a dog would pay for a kennel in London today.)

The Duke of Chandos had his own orchestra of 27 musicians while Sir Robert Walpole spent £1,500 a year on wine (£90,000 today) and £1 every night on candles, (the miserable could buy food, drink, fuel and shelter for five weeks for that £1).

BUT ... the 'great' needed the votes of the lower classes when it came to elections for parliament. They had to invite the farmers into their great homes! Yeuch! The Earl of Cork whinged...

> *At election time I have to open my doors to every dirty fellow in the county who has a vote. All my best floors are spoiled by the hobnailed boots of the farmers stamping about them. Every room is a pigsty and the Chinese wallpaper in the drawing room stinks so terrible of tobacco that it would knock you down to walk into it.*

Poor Earl of Cork!

Posh politics

The posh Georgians in Britain sent people to 'Parliament' to argue with the king. Where did this Parliament thing come from? Here's a quick horrible history...

♚ The first big argument was in 1215 when the posh people of England (the Barons) fell out with King John. They made him sign a great charter (posh name: Magna Carta). This said he couldn't have everything his own way just because he was king. John sulked but he signed.

♚ Then along came King Henry III who forgot all about the Magna Carta and started demanding money. So one of the Barons, Simon de Montfort, organized a group of Barons to talk about horrible Henry. They talked in French ('cos they was posh). French for 'to talk' is parler so a talk-shop is 'parler-ment' or Parliament. Geddit?

♚ Simple Simon went to war with Henry. He lost at the Battle of Evesham and had his head cut off – not to mention his arms and his legs! But his Parliament idea lived on.

♚ Members of Parliament (MPs for short) were the chief men of the towns and counties. The rich men voted for them and sent them to argue with the kings and queens. (Women, even rich, posh women, had no say at all.) Sometimes the MPs got really angry and turned nasty – in 1647 they went to war with King Charles I and ended up cutting his head off.

♚ The last Stuart Queen, Anne, enjoyed going to Parliament and listening to them talk. But she didn't argue with them very much. The situation was desperate! Who on earth could they argue with? They began to argue with each other, and split up into two parties – one lot were nicknamed the 'Whigs' and the other lot were called the 'Tories'. These were actually very insulting names. A 'Whig' was a Scottish robber who usually murdered his victim, while a 'Tory' was an Irish cattle thief. The queen cheated a bit to make sure her favourites, the Tories, stayed in power.

That brings us to the gorgeous Georgians…

Potty parties

Disaster! King George I didn't do a lot of arguing with his Parliament because he hardly spoke any English. He gave a lot of presents and power to the Whigs and they ruled the country for him. The Tories hated George I – they only supported him because they thought he was better than the Catholic James Stuart. Even the Whigs didn't like him much!

Parliament now had the power!

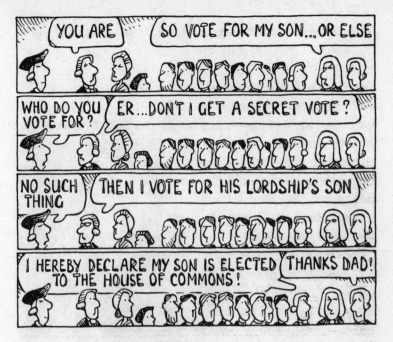

There were more Lords' sons in the House of Commons than any other group.

Did you know…?

- Some places had so few voters they could be paid to vote the way someone wanted – they were called 'rotten boroughs'.
- Some of the growing factory towns couldn't send anyone to Parliament at all.
- Some places were run by a powerful family who could send anyone to Parliament they liked – these were known as 'pocket boroughs'.
- MPs weren't paid. Only rich men could afford to be MPs. Who would they stick up for in Parliament? Their rich friends, of course.

The way Britain picked its politicians was unfair and potty. No wonder the Georgians got so many…

Peculiar prime ministers
Wily Walpole

One man whose family ran a pocket borough was Sir Robert Walpole. He is the man that historians call the first prime minister – King George I's top dog in the House of Commons.

But the title prime minister was an insult! It meant 'King George's favourite creep in parliament'. (It's a bit like someone calling you a teacher's pet!) So Robert Walpole said, 'I am NOT a prime minister.' Then he went on not being a prime minister for the next 21 years.

He had a good way to make sure he won every vote in parliament. He paid the MPs to vote the way he wanted.

EVERY MAN HAS HIS PRICE

This is dishonest – Britain got the laws that the rich paid for, not the laws that the poor needed – but no one seemed to mind too much.

Poorly Pitt

William Pitt (the Elder) – PM in 1757 – was dead honest. He did not believe in bribing MPs, unlike Walpole. But he did find the job a strain. He became almost mad with the strain and the cure was to lock him in a darkened room. His wife passed food through to him.

Being half mad didn't stop George III being king and it didn't stop Pitt being prime minister. They let him out of the room to speak in the House of Lords. This was a big mistake. While he was speaking he collapsed and died.

No-good North

Lord North – PM in 1770 – has been called the worst prime minister ever. He soon got bored in Parliament and would nod off to sleep. He'd ask to be woken up when the speaker got to the end. He was also the ugliest prime minister Britain has ever had.

Lord North often complained that it was a terrible strain being prime minister…

> *I'd rather be hanged than suffer the pain of running the king's business.*

So, how did he get the job? When he was a boy he was a playmate of King George III, so George gave him the PM job.

Portable Pitt
William Pitt (the Younger) – PM from 1783 – was honest like his dear departed Dad. And, like his Dad, was pretty miserable in his job. He was the youngest prime minister ever at the age of 24.

He led Britain through many of its years of war with France. He made the proud boast…

> *I can save this country, and no one else can.*

He did this by raising new taxes. He put a tax on houses with more than seven windows – some grumpy Georgians just bricked up the extra windows to dodge the tax! But as he lay ill in 1806 he heard that Napoleon had battered the Brit armies at Austerlitz and he groaned…

> *Oh, my country. How I leave my country!*

The man who'd boasted, 'I can save my country' did the most sensible thing possible. He died straight after saying those words.

42

He broke another record: he became the youngest prime minister ever to *die* in office when he popped his parliamentary clogs at the age of 46. It wasn't the darkened room that killed this Pitt but the bottles of port wine he swilled.

Potted Perceval

Spencer Perceval – PM in 1812 – was about as popular as the plague. A man called Bellingham was imprisoned in Russia and lost all his money. Bellingham thought the British government should give him back the money he'd lost. The government said, 'No.' Bellingham said, 'Right! I'll show you!' and he took a pistol into the House of Commons where he shot PM Perceval dead. He's the only British PM ever to be assassinated.

Crowds came out onto the street to cheer, 'Perceval is dead! Hurrah!'

Pretty soon Bellingham was dead too because he was hanged. (This was cheaper than paying him the money he wanted.)

Prime ministers have their famous last words recorded by historians for teachers to bore you with. At least PM Perceval left us with a nice short final speech:

Cheerless for children

One of the worst classes to be in was the 'children's' class.

Children were dressed as adults and often worked as adults from a very early age. The hard part was surviving childhood…

1 First you had to survive being born. One child out of three didn't live to be 15, and careless mothers cost babies' lives. There were many cases of a baby sharing a bed with mother, father, brothers or sisters and being smothered when someone rolled on top of them in their sleep.

IF YOUR FATHER ROLLED OVER HE'D SMOTHER THE LOT OF US!

SNORE

2 Poor families could not afford too many children. There were cases of babies being left in the streets to die, or strangled and dumped on the local rubbish tip or into a drain.

3 Next you had to survive your christening. At a christening in Surrey a nurse got very drunk. She undressed the baby and went to put it in its cradle. By mistake she put it too close to a large fire which killed it in a few minutes. She told the judges who tried her that she thought the baby was a log of firewood. The judges set her free! (Georgian judges were often drunk in court. The nurse's judges must have been if they thought a baby and a log could be mistaken!

YOU CAN SLEEP LIKE A LOG AND SLEEP LIKE A BABY, EASY TO MIX 'EM UP

They probably said, 'She was so drunk she wooden know the difference.')

4 A child who was brought up by a paid child-minder, a 'nurse', was unlucky. Children with nurses were twice as likely to die. Nurses were well known for being drunk. Nurses of poor children often deliberately damaged the child's face or legs so the child would grow up to be a more pitiful sight. The nurse would then hire out the child to a beggar who would make more money.

5 Thomas Coram opened a hospital for unwanted children in 1741. He was flooded with so many sick and dying babies, dumped on the doorstep, that about 10,000 of the children died. But his good example led the later Georgians to look after poor children better.

6 Young girls in rich homes had to grow up to be ladies with fine figures. That meant having a narrow waist. Some were fitted with a steel cage under their clothes that pinched their stomachs in. The pinching went a little too far with Elizabeth Evelyn. She died. Elizabeth was *two* years old!

7 Orphans could have a terribly tough time. To keep large numbers of them quiet at night they'd be given a mixture called Godfrey's cordial which was full of the powerful drug opium.

It sent them to sleep all right – but give them too much and they didn't wake up … ever!

8 Children were often taken from orphanages to become servants. But Elizabeth Brownrigg treated them more like slaves. Girls were kept in filthy cellars, left in the cold with no clothes and constantly whipped. They slept on rotten straw and were given scraps to eat. Of course many girls died after this sort of treatment. Then one escaped and reported Elizabeth Brownrigg to the parish officers. They visited the Brownrigg house and found another girl on the point of death. They arrested Brownrigg and she was hanged.

9 Then you had to survive school. Some poor children went to 'dame' schools run by a local woman or to 'charity' schools, paid for by rich people in the area. But 'public' schools, where rich parents paid to send their children, were in a dreadful state in Georgian times. Teachers were violent and pupils were worse! A boy wrote home to complain about his life in the bedrooms: 'I have been woken up many times by the hot points of cigars burning holes in my face.'

MORNING, SMITHERS

10 But children *did* fight back! In 1793 there was a 'Great Rebellion' at Winchester school. The boys took over a tower at the school and refused to come down. The gentle boys threw stones at the teachers below – the not-so-gentle ones

fired pistols! At the same school in 1818 a pupil rebellion had to be dealt with by soldiers using bayonets.

NAPOLEON'S CAVALRY IS ONE THING, BUT ARMED ANGRY PUBLIC SCHOOLBOYS ARE QUITE ANOTHER

BANG

POP

Did you know…?

One of Winchester's old pupils, Thomas Arnold, went as head teacher to Rugby School and wrote the famous book *Tom Brown's School Days* about life there. But Rugby had its own problems before Arnold got the job there. In 1797 a gang of pupils used gunpowder to blow up the headmaster's door! (And you thought you were daring when you dropped a stink-bomb in school assembly?)

Wild women

Being a child wasn't fun – but it was probably worse being a woman. Men expected their wives to be quiet and to obey them. But there were times when a bit of wildness in a woman came in handy.

In Georgian times it was women who went to market to buy the corn. If the price of corn was too high then their families would go hungry. And it was the women who bullied the farmers into cutting their prices.

The wild women of Bewdley, for example, cut open sacks of wheat and told the farmers they would only pay what people were paying in nearby towns. The women won.

In Exeter, the townsmen heard that farmers were going to put up the prices of corn. They sent their women to market to argue for a lower price ... or 'take it by force'! The women won again.

In Bewdley and Exeter the men were happy to stand back and send the women to battle for the food.

Of course, women were not treated so well when it came to work and pay ... especially pay. Women worked as hard as men in the farmers' fields – but they were paid half as much. Then, when farm jobs were short, it was the women who got the sack.

But what was it like for Georgian women? Test your brain-power with this simple test. Which of these foul facts were true for woeful Georgian women?

1 Georgian men believed that women were not as intelligent as they were.

2 Georgian girls married when they were just 12 years old.

3 A woman who killed her husband could be burned alive as a punishment.

4 Some men would get rid of a wife by selling her at an auction.

SHE WAS WORTH A LOT MORE THAN I THOUGHT SHE WAS

5 A husband who beat his wife would be punished.

6 Women used arsenic poison to make themselves look beautiful.

7 In the middle of the 1700s a hard-working man in industry could earn £3 a week – a maidservant in a house would earn £3 *a year*!

MAYBE I SHOULD JUST AUCTION MYSELF INSTEAD

8 Lady Wortley Montague was famous for being the cleanest woman in Britain.

9 A woman could be divorced if she'd used make-up to trick a man into marrying her.

EEK!

IF YOU WANT TO SELL HER, PUT THE MAKE-UP BACK ON

10 Fashionable women wore masks to keep the sun off their faces.

Answers:

1 True. That's what they believed. Of course they were wrong. Women were every bit as intelligent as men but were not given a good education and didn't have the chance to show how clever they were.

EVEN IF YOU HAD AN EDUCATION, WE WOULD STILL BE MORE INTELLIGENTER

2 False. The average age was about 24. Very few married at under 16 but there is a curious report of a Christchurch parson who married a girl of 13. He was 83 years old at the time. But he was seriously weird. He was a rich man who dressed so carelessly he was often mistaken for a tramp.

3 True. A man murdering his wife was hanged but women could be burned. In 1726, Catherine Hayes was sentenced to die at the stake. The 'kind' judges decided she would be strangled first so she didn't suffer death by burning. But the flames were lit too soon and the executioner couldn't reach her to kill her quickly. In Maidstone in 1769 Susannah Lott died at the stake before she was burned and didn't suffer so much. This law was finally changed in 1789 so women got equal rights – the right to be hanged for murder.

4 True. It was not legal but it sometimes happened. The woman was taken to market with a rope round her neck and sold to the highest bidder. Sometimes a woman would fetch a few pounds and sometimes she could be traded for an ox – better for pulling a plough, of course, but it didn't make such a good cup of tea. This uncommon sort of divorce was last heard of in 1887.

5 False. A husband was allowed to beat his wife. The stick he used must be no thicker than his thumb, so he could whip her with a cane but probably not a walking stick.

6 True. The white powder was put on the skin to make it pale and smooth and beautiful. If too much of the white poison got into your mouth you'd be pale and smooth and dead. This happened to a famous beauty, Maria Gunning in the 1750s. (She was warned!) There was also poisonous mercury and lead in some of this make-up which could make you go bald. And it was a mistake to kiss these women! There was a scandal in Italy when over 600 men died from getting too close to wives wearing arsenic make-up!

7 True. A mirror in a great house like Holkham Hall, Norfolk, was said to have cost £500. If a £3-a-year maid broke that mirror then the owners would have to stop her wages for 166 years and eight months to pay for it.

8 False. Lady Wortley Montague was filthy. She was once told that her hands were rather dirty. She replied, 'If you think they are dirty then you ought to see my feet!'

9 True. In 1770 the British government passed a law saying a woman who tricked a man with make-up was as bad as a witch. If he married her, and found she was ugly underneath all the powder and paint, then he could be un-married any time he wanted.

10 True. A pale skin was beautiful to the Georgians. A mask in front of the face would protect the skin. Of course it was awkward trying to hold a mask up so some had a button attached to the back and the button was held between the teeth. These masks had eye cut-outs so were suntanned eyeballs all right?

Gruesome Georgians

Georgian Britain was a prime crime time. In 1700 there were about 50 crimes that could be punished by death. By 1822 they had lost count! There were at least 200 hanging crimes and some experts believe there were as many as 350! These included...

- Going armed in disguise (so the Lone Ranger would have been in trouble).
- Poaching fish (but a poached egg was fine).
- Forging bank notes (but not sick notes to teachers, so you'd have been safe).[1]
- Cutting down trees (with criminals rooted out by the men of Special Branch).

And, of course, murder...

The mystery of the moors

Daniel Clarke was a Yorkshire shoemaker who married a wealthy woman. The trouble was he liked to boast about his riches. 'I'm the richest man in Knaresborough! You should see my jewels!'

On 8 February 1745 he disappeared, never to be seen alive again.

Law officers found some of Clarke's jewels in the house of a man called Eugene Aram. Aram was arrested but said Clarke had given them to him before he left the county. The magistrates had to let Eugene Aram go free.

Of course, as you may have guessed, Aram had murdered Clarke and stolen the jewels. Not only did he get away with it, but he got to keep the jewels and he moved to Kings Lynn in Norfolk. He had got away with murder! Until...

1. In 1820, 46 people were hanged for forging banknotes. But after the executions, some of the notes were shown to be genuine. Oops!

Fourteen years later a labourer was digging for limestone in a cave when he came across some human bones. No one could prove that they were the bones of Daniel Clarke, but Eugene Aram was arrested anyway. He was found guilty and hanged. His body was hung in a cage by the Knaresborough road where the murder happened. As the body rotted, and the bones fell through the bars of the cage, his widow was allowed to pick them up. But one night a doctor took the skull and it's still on view in the Royal College of Surgeons' Museum in London.

Gruesome!

So here's the mystery. What sort of man would murder the shoemaker for his money? Can you guess? Was Eugene Aram…

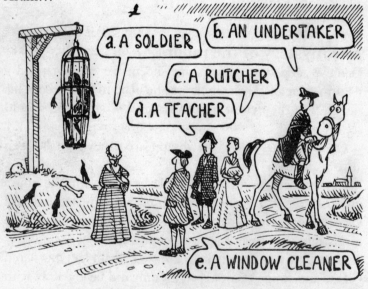

a. A SOLDIER
b. AN UNDERTAKER
c. A BUTCHER
d. A TEACHER
e. A WINDOW CLEANER

Answer: d) Eugene Aram was an English teacher. Which just goes to show … something!

Heroes and villains

The Georgians had some pretty famous villains. The trouble is they became heroes, a bit like Robin Hood. You know the sort of thing...

Take smugglers, for example. Georgian Britain was a time for smuggling. Lots of people seemed to think they were doing a good job – half the tea drunk in Britain was smuggled in to the country. Lace was smuggled in – stuffed inside geese; brandy kegs were hidden inside lobster pots; tobacco was twisted into ropes and hidden amongst the ropes used on the ships.

All good fun and part of the game called 'cheat-the-government'. Smugglers today are seen as brave outlaws. You probably know the poem by Rudyard Kipling...

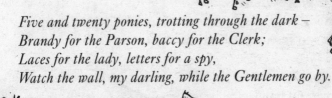

Five and twenty ponies, trotting through the dark –
Brandy for the Parson, baccy for the Clerk;
Laces for the lady, letters for a spy,
Watch the wall, my darling, while the Gentlemen go by.

The trouble was these 'gentlemen' were nasty, cruel and greedy. They'd probably cut your throat just for the fun of it and then say, 'You still think I'm a hero?'

In 1748 a man called Chater betrayed a smuggling gang and a law officer called Galley tried to arrest them. A magazine of the time described what happened next…

They began with poor Galley, cut off his nose, broke every joint of him and after several hours of torture dispatched him. Chater they carried to a dry well, hung him by the middle to a cross beam in it, leaving him to perish with hunger and pain. But when they came, several days after, and heard him groan, they cut the rope, let him drop to the bottom and threw in logs and stones to cover him. The person who told the magistrates the story was in disguise because he feared the same would happen to him.

Some 'gentlemen' they turned out to be.

Never mind the story books and poems. Here is the terrible truth about these exciting criminals!

The highwayman
Name: Dick Turpin (also called himself John Palmer)
Claim to fame: Highwayman
Life: 1705 – 1739
The story:
• Brave and handsome hero who was a wonderful rider.
• He robbed stage coaches but was always very polite … especially to ladies.
• He rode his gallant horse, Black Bess, all the way from

Essex to York in record time to prove he couldn't have committed a crime ... though he had.

The terrible truth:

- He was a butcher boy till he decided there was more money in stealing cattle than chopping them. He joined 'The Essex Gang' of violent house-breakers. They entered someone's home, robbed it and tortured the occupants till they handed over their money and valuables.
- When most of the Gang was arrested Turpin tried his hand at a different crime. He stopped a gentleman on the road and threatened him with a pistol. That man was Tom King, the famous highwayman. King took Turpin as a partner. They spent two years terrorizing the Essex roads. When King was caught Turpin tried to rescue him but accidentally shot his partner dead!
- Turpin was arrested for stealing sheep in Yorkshire. No one knew he was the famous highwayman until his old teacher recognized his handwriting! Turpin ended up hanged in York. He never made the famous ride on Black Bess – though another highwayman, John Nevison, may have done.

Not to be confused with: Black Beauty, Turnip Townsend, Mashed Turnip.

The outlaw

Name: Rob Roy MacGregor (also known as Red Roy or Robert the Red. When he joined the English he changed his name to Robert Campbell.)

Claim to fame: Outlaw

Life: 1671 – 1734

The story:

- Poor Rob was the Scottish Robin Hood. He was outlawed just because he was from the clan MacGregor, not because he was a criminal. For years he lived in caves and woods, often escaping the law by the skin of his teeth.

- He led his poor neighbours in their struggle against cattle thieves from the north. Rob Roy led them to freedom from the terror.

- He fought bravely for his country in their struggle against the English.

The terrible truth:

- A cattle thief by the age of 20. He fought for Scotland in the Glorious Revolution against England – but switched sides when he saw he was going to lose.

- Became a respectable cattle dealer but, when times got hard, he took his customers' money and ran off with it to the Western Isles.

- While he lived as a bandit he threatened cattle owners: 'Pay me to leave your cattle alone.' Switched sides again and fought against the English but was captured. King George pardoned him. He went home to live a quiet life.

Not to be confused with: Red Rum, Roy of the Rovers.

The pirate
Name: Blackbeard (full name Edward Teach, also known as Tache or Thatch – though he was christened Edward Drummond)
Claim to fame: Pirate
Life: Born in Bristol, date unknown, died 1718
The story:

- Blackbeard went into battle with six pistols at his waist and lighted matches under his hat to make him look frightening. (He was a bit of a hot-head.)

- He was a brave English hero who stole from the French. His treasure was buried on a desert island and no one has found it to this day.

- Blackbeard died fighting against a small army. When his body was thrown into the sea it swam round the ship three times before it sank.

The terrible truth:

- Blackbeard was a vicious bully. He went into business with the Governor of North Carolina in America. The Governor let Blackbeard attack ships – any ships, not just the French – so long as he got a share of the loot.

- The 'treasure' wasn't gold and jewels but goods like barrels of sugar. The American people (not the French) became so fed up with Blackbeard they sent a naval ship to stop him.

- In a hand-to-hand battle Lieutenant Robert Maynard shot Blackbeard dead – then cut his head off just to make sure.

Not to be confused with: Bluebeard, King Edward potatoes, teachers called Edward, Margaret Thatcher, Black Bess, Black Beauty, black pudding – and there's no truth in the story that his crew said a Teach should be nicknamed Blackboard!

And, talking about pirates…

Pirates, parrots and eye-patches

Have you ever seen a film about pirates? They were funny old characters, and liked a good laugh and a quick chorus of 'Fifteen men on a dead man's chest, yo-ho-ho and a bottle of rum!' Then they battled bravely against huge Spanish galleons and made the cowardly captains cough up some terrific treasure.

Right?

Wrong.

Here is the terrible truth about the gorgeous Georgian pirates:

1 Spanish treasure ships By Georgian times there were no Francis Drake characters attacking Spanish galleons and winning gold for England and the Queen. They attacked little trading ships to steal tobacco or slaves or just spare sails and anchor cable. ('Your anchor cable or your life?' doesn't sound so gorgeous, does it?)

2 Head-scarves Did they really tie large, coloured handkerchiefs round their heads? Yes. (If you want to try this then use a clean hankie. 'Snot very nice otherwise.)

3 Walking the plank Have you ever seen the play *Peter Pan*? Cut-throat Captain Hook plans to make the Lost Boys walk the plank and drop off into crocodile-infested waters. Very dramatic. But true? No. Pirates couldn't be bothered with that sort of play-acting. Some cruel pirates did tell their captives, 'You're free to walk home!' while they were in the middle of shark-filled seas. If they wanted to get rid of their victims then they just hacked them to death and threw them over the side. (That's a bit boring – especially for the victim, who'd be bored to death – but it saved a lot of time.)

4 Marooning Did they really leave a sailor on some desert island with a bottle of water and a gun? Yes, they did. It was a punishment usually kept for pirates who tried to desert their shipmates. The most famous marooned sailor was Alexander Selkirk whose adventures were turned into the story *Robinson Crusoe*. (Imagine being alone and lonely with no friendly human to talk to. You'd go mad. And teachers are still doing this today. They call it detention.)

5 The Jolly Roger flag Did pirates fly the black flag with a white skull and crossbones? Sometimes. Most Tudor and Stuart pirates flew a red flag – they put a story around that the flag was dyed with blood. Georgian pirates started to come up with their own designs. (What picture would you have on your flag to strike terror into the hearts of your enemies? A school and cross boys, perhaps.)

HOW DO YOU SUPPOSE THAT IS GOING TO STRIKE TERROR INTO THE HEARTS OF OUR ENEMIES?

6 Wooden legs Did pirates limp around on wooden legs? Some did. Fighting against the cannon of naval vessels was dangerous, and legs, arms and heads must have flown around like skittles in a bowling alley. Of course they didn't have doctors on board to make a neat job of a mangled arm or leg – but the ship's carpenter could carve you a neat replacement.

7 Parrots Did pirates have parrots on their shoulders? Not usually – but they often carried them in cages back to Britain from South America. They could teach them to speak during the voyage back across the Atlantic then sell them as pets in Britain.

8 Buried treasure Much more money has been spent *searching* for pirate treasure than has ever been *found*. If you won a million on the lottery would you bury it? No, you'd want to spend it. So did the pirates. Was there ever such a place as Treasure Island? The writer Robert Louis Stevenson spent a wet holiday in Scotland in 1881 and painted a map of an island for fun. He named it Skeleton Island and liked it so much he wrote the book *Treasure Island* to go with the map. Stevenson never met a pirate and he pinched the 'Dead man's chest' song from another writer's book.

9 Keel hauling A pirate found guilty of a crime against the crew would be forced to swallow cockroaches – if he was lucky! If he was unlucky he'd be *keel hauled*. A rope was tied under his arms and another to his feet. He was thrown into the sea and dragged under the bottom of the boat ('hauled' under the 'keel'). He might survive drowning but there were very rough barnacles clinging to the bottom of a wooden ship that would scrape the skin. (And, when he got back, the rotten crew didn't even give him an Elastoplast!)

10 Gold earrings Did tough pirates wear pretty gold rings in their ears? Yes! They were a superstitious lot and believed that a gold earring gave them better eye sight. (A pirate never wore glasses, because he didn't want to make a spectacle of himself.)

Painful punishments

Georgians tried to be tough on criminals. Hangings were performed in public so everyone could see what happened to naughty boys and girls.

Of course the Georgian newspapers loved crime stories as much as today's papers. Here are some genuine press cuttings…

Fortune-telling

A local record book records a curious crime and a cruel punishment in the north of England…

Susannah Fleming stood in the pillory at White Cross for an hour for fortune-telling. Though she was not bothered by the public she was nearly strangled either because she fainted or because her neck was held too tightly. A sailor, out of kindness, brought her down the ladder on his back in nearly a dying state.

Suicide

The Georgians thought they were wiser than the people of the Middle Ages and Tudor times. But old superstitions lingered on.

Killing yourself was against the law, so it had to be punished. How do you punish people who have killed themselves? The Georgians had no problem. *The Western Flying Post* newspaper reported the death of an old man in 1755...

On 6 June an old man hanged himself by his handkerchief at Linkincehorn in Cornwall. The coroner decided that he had committed suicide. He was buried at Kesbrook Crossroad and a stake driven through his body.

A suicide victim could not be buried in a churchyard because, the Georgians said, he had gone against God's law. He was buried at the crossroads so the ghost would be confused about which way to go to get back home. Why a stake through his body? Because people believed this would stop the man rising from his grave and haunting the area.

Sheep-stealing

Stealing a sheep could be punished by hanging in Georgian times – a 12 year-old boy was sentenced to death for stealing a lamb in 1802. But one sheep thief saved the law officers a rope! He stole a sheep and managed to hang himself. In 1762 the *Gloucester Journal* reported…

On Tuesday afternoon a man was found strangled in a field. He had stolen a sheep and, to carry it away, had tied the back legs and put the cord over his head. When he rested on a gate the sheep kicked, the cord dropped over his neck and strangled him.

At least he died with a *sheepish* grin on his face. The good news is the sheep lived. The bad news is it was certainly eaten by someone else not long after.

Did you know…?
Prison in Georgian times was not like prison today. Prisoners could keep pets. But in 1714, Newgate Prison in London banned one of the most popular pets: pigs.

Witchcraft

The ancient way of testing for witchcraft was to throw a suspect into water and see if they floated – a witch would float (be taken out, hanged and die) while an innocent person would sink (probably drown and die anyway).

Ruth Osborne was beaten and drowned at Tring in 1751 as a suspected witch. Twenty years later, in the same town, a man and his wife both suffered the 'water ordeal' – the woman died and the man *just* survived.

But things were changing. In 1770 a man accused a 55-year-old woman of witchcraft. She said, 'I don't think I'm a witch – but you'd better try me, just to make sure!' The *Northampton Mercury* newspaper described what happened…

A miller in the area was chosen to perform the ducking ceremony. The poor woman went to the mill where a great number of people were gathered. The miller remembered what had happened in Tring and refused to try her in front of such a large crowd. He promised he would try her, in secret, as soon as he was alone.

The crowd left. The woman survived. We can guess that the miller didn't try too hard to drown her. Wise man. Maybe the Georgians were learning some common sense after all.

Theft

Any sort of theft was punished very harshly in Georgian times. In Norwich a girl was hanged for stealing a petticoat. No one seemed to object, though the girl was just seven years old.

Bodies for sale

Wild life, wilder death

Jonathan Wild was a thief-taker. He promised to find your stolen goods for you … if you paid him a reward, of course.

People came to him from all over London. 'Can you get back my stolen property?' they asked.

'I'll leave messages in certain places,' he said. 'The thieves will leave your stolen goods where I can find them. I will leave them a reward. Everybody's happy.'

'You are wonderful, Mr Wild.'

'I know,' he said.

The truth was that Jonathan Wild had organized the robbery in the first place! No wonder he knew how to get the stolen property back. In time every thief in London was working for Wild and every victim in London came to him for help.

No thief dared to upset Wild because Wild would simply betray the thief to the law. He had 75 criminals convicted and 60 of those were hanged.

Wild grew rich and fat. By 1724 he was in complete control of London crime. But in the end Wild's wickedness was uncovered and he was hanged. Thousands gathered to pelt him with mud and stones as he was taken to the gallows.

Yet Wild still had some friends left and they did a curious thing. They smuggled his dead body away and buried it in a secret place at the dead of night. Why would they do such a thing? Because they were afraid William Cheselden would get his hands on the body. Mr Cheselden was a surgeon and he was interested in learning about the human body by cutting up dead ones. (He was also interested in cutting up live ones but they wouldn't let him!)

Where did Mr Cheselden get his dead bodies from?

He bought bodies of criminals who'd been hanged. That's what Wild's friends were afraid of.

Did Cheselden get Wild's body? Yes. The secret grave was found, the body was dug up and delivered to the surgeon. (The skeleton of Wild can still be seen today in the Hunterian Museum at the Royal College of Surgeons if you are sick-minded enough to want to look at it.)

The age of the bodysnatcher had begun!

'Better get back in your coffin, mate!' – a gorgeous Georgian tale of terror

Edward Henson was crying and the tears spilled into his ale. 'You're pathetic,' the landlord said. 'You're drunk.'

'I'm not,' Edward argued but his voice was slurred and his eyes were rolling in his leather-skinned face.

'I've seen a lot of drunks in my time and I tell you, sailor, you're drunk. You don't even know that you're crying into your beer,' the landlord sneered, wiping a greasy hand on his stained apron.

The air of the quayside tavern was smoky with

69

the cheap tallow candles and shadows hid the filth on the floor. 'I'm sad,' Edward moaned.

'You'll get no more ale in this tavern,' the landlord said firmly.

'No! Listen. I had a friend. The best friend a man ever had. His name was Geordie. Poor Geordie.'

Edward took a deep drink of the clouded drink and wiped his mouth on the back of his sleeve, then he wiped his nose, then he wiped his eyes. 'He's dead.'

'I'm sorry,' the landlord said. 'What did he die of?'

'Don't know. I'm not a doctor. He woke up yesterday morning and he was dead!' the sailor said.

'These things happen,' the landlord shrugged.

'I went to Geordie's funeral this afternoon. Sort of said goodbye to him. We've sailed together for ten years or more. All over the world.'

The landlord slipped onto the bench alongside the drunken sailor and lowered his voice. 'I hope he rests in peace,' he said.

'He will, he will. He'll go straight to heaven, will Geordie.'

'I'm sure his soul will go to heaven,' the landlord said. 'It's his body I'd worry about.'

'His body? It's dead. I saw it myself! I said, "You're quiet this morning Geordie," and he never replied. That's because he was dead, you know. Did I tell you he was dead?'

The landlord grabbed the sailor's arm and shook him. 'The sack-'em-up men are in this town.'

'Shack-'em who?'

'Sack-'em-up men! Bodysnatchers! In the past six weeks we've lost five bodies from the local churchyard.'

'Lost them? How can you lose a body?'

'They were dug up, put in a sack and taken to the hospital.'

'So the doctors could make them better?' Edward said cheerfully. 'Will they make my friend Geordie better?'

'No! The doctors want to cut them up. To try their experiments on. If you don't want your friend to end up on a doctor's table then you'd better go and have a look at the grave tonight. But be careful. These sack-'em-up men aren't too fussy about what they take. If they catch you interfering they'll slap a pitch plaster over your mouth to shut you up.'

'A pitch plaster? I'll suffocate!' the sailor cried.

'Then that'll save them digging up your friend,' the landlord warned. 'Most people watch their friends' graves in groups of four or five. Some people even sleep near the graves for two or three weeks.'

'Two or three weeks?'

'Till the body's too rotten to be any use to the doctors,' the landlord explained.

'My ship sails in two days,' Edward moaned.

'But tonight's the night when the sack-'em-up men will be after him.' The landlord took the sailor's ale tankard and helped him to his feet. Out of the door, turn right and climb

the hill. 'The churchyard's on your right. It's behind the high wall.'

Edward Henson looked almost sober as he said, 'Thank you. I'll go and look after Geordie.'

He staggered towards the door, crashing against tables and upsetting tankards. The night air was damp and there was a light, chill mist blurring the moon. Edward took a few deep breaths and used the wall to guide himself along the muddy lane that ran along the river front.

The mist seemed to deaden the sounds of the night. All the sailor could hear was the squish of his boots in the mud and his own creaking breathing. The pie stall at the end of Low Row was closed. Two men had been there earlier in the night with their cheerful cries of 'Chelsea buns!', 'Pies all smoking hot!' and 'Mutton pies!' Edward suddenly realized that he was hungry. He turned away from the deserted pie stall and up the hill. He passed the small stone prison cell at the foot of Crown Street and left behind the pitiful sobbing of its solitary prisoner.

After ten minutes he reached a high wall that was soft and slimy to the touch with the moss that grew on it. In the faint moonlight he saw a white shape looming ahead of him. He strained his eyes and at last made out the shape of a man. A man dressed in a white night shirt. A rope was fastened under his armpits and he was hanging over the churchyard wall by the rope.

Edward blinked. He took a few steps towards the figure then stopped. The face was ghastly but he knew it.

'Geordie!' he cried. 'It's you, Geordie!'

Geordie didn't reply.

The sailor reached out a hand and grasped the wrist of his friend. 'My, but you're cold, Geordie!' he said. 'It's not like you to be out on a chilly night like this dressed in your nightgown.'

Geordie didn't reply.

Edward Henson rubbed a hand over his eyes. 'Oh, but I was forgetting! You died yesterday! You'd better get back in your coffin, mate, before you catch your death of cold!'

Suddenly the rope went tight and a moment later the

corpse was whisked back over the graveyard wall. There was a muttered conversation and footsteps padding over the grass behind the wall.

Edward straightened his shoulders and seemed suddenly sober. He hurried to the house that stood at the gateway to the graveyard. He rapped on the heavy oak door. A window rattled open. 'Who's there?'

'It's me.'

'Who's me?'

'Edward Henson, from the collier ship *Cushie Butterfield*.'

'What do you want?'

'Are you in charge of this graveyard?'

'I am.'

'Well, I'm here to tell you the dead 'uns are getting out of the churchyard!'

There was a roar of anger from the man at the window. It slammed shut and he was down at the door a few minutes later. He ran out with a gun and vanished between the shadowy gravestones. Edward Henson heard shots and cries.

He walked wearily up the hill to his lodging house. Without bothering to undress he fell onto his straw mattress next to a snoring sailor, pulled a rough wool blanket over himself and was asleep in no time.

The next night he was drinking his ale a lot more slowly.

'So you saved your friend from the sack-'em-up men, I hear,' the landlord said. He was looking at Edward Henson with a little more respect tonight.

'I did. And I hear they found a trail of blood in the churchyard this morning,' the sailor said. 'They do say the bodysnatchers won't be back in this town for a while.'

'Then I owe you a drink, my friend,' the landlord grinned.

'I'd rather have a bite to eat.' There were no pies on sale tonight.

The landlord leaned forward, his thick hands planted heavily on the wet table. 'They do say the two pie men have vanished. A funny couple of men. Foreigners. From Scotland.'

'Ah!'

'And that pie stall was in the perfect place to watch everything that went on in the churchyard.'

'You mean…'

'It looks like they may have been the bodysnatchers.'

Edward Henson shuddered and took a long drink of his ale. 'You say they sold the bodies to the doctors?'

'They did. They got four guineas apiece for fresh ones. The doctors can't get enough of them. Why?'

The sailor shook his head and looked into the dregs of his ale. 'I was just wondering about their tasty mutton pies…'

Would you make a good bodysnatcher?

The three leading members of a Scottish bodysnatching gang were known as The Spoon, The Mole, and Merry Andrew. Merry Andrew cheated the other two out of some bodysnatching money and they were angry. They planned their revenge. Merry Andrew's sister, Sarah, had just died and they planned to snatch her body and sell it to the doctors.

Imagine you are Merry Andrew. You guess what your partners are up to. What are you going to do about it…

a) You can report The Spoon and The Mole to the law officers. A watch will be kept on your dear sister's grave. As soon as the bodysnatching villains appear, the law officers will appear and stop them, Sarah can rest in peace and the wicked plan is ruined.

b) You can watch the graveyard. When The Mole and The Spoon appear you can go off to fetch the law officers. The bodysnatchers will be caught in the act. They will have sweated for nothing and they will probably go to jail. Poor beloved Sarah will have been disturbed, but it is worth it to see them locked away.

c) You can hide in the graveyard alone. When The Spoon and The Mole have dug up your sister you can leap out of hiding, dressed in a white sheet, pretending to be a ghost and scare them off. You can put your sister back and cover up her grave again. The villains won't be back and Sarah will be safe.

d) You can hide in the graveyard alone. When The Spoon and The Mole have dug up your sister you can leap out of hiding, dressed in a white sheet, pretending to be a ghost and scare them off. You can take your darling Sarah's body to the surgeon and sell her. The Mole and the Spoon have done the work, you collect the money ... if you can bear to sell your own sister, of course.

Which of the above would you do?
Which did Merry Andrew do?

Answer: **d)** Merry Andrew sold his sister's body to the surgeons. He even chased The Mole and The Spoon away from the cart they had waiting. He borrowed it to get his sister to the surgeon. He enjoyed telling the story and always had a good laugh. 'The Spoon went without his porridge that night!' he'd chuckle.

If you answered **d)**, and you have a sister, then someone should warn her about you!

Quaint quack doctors

The more bodies the doctors cut up the more they learned about the human body. But there was still a lot of ignorance about sickness and disease and many people still took curious cures for their problems.

Newspapers were packed with adverts for curious cures. The following advert is invented but the cures offered are all real Georgian medicines.

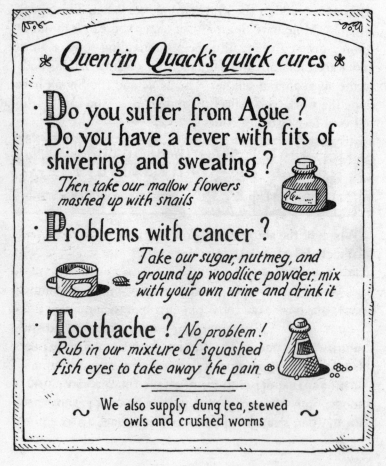

✳ Quentin Quack's quick cures ✳

· **D**o you suffer from Ague?
Do you have a fever with fits of shivering and sweating?
Then take our mallow flowers mashed up with snails

· **P**roblems with cancer?
Take our sugar, nutmeg, and ground up woodlice powder, mix with your own urine and drink it

· **T**oothache? *No problem!*
Rub in our mixture of squashed fish eyes to take away the pain ✿

~ We also supply dung tea, stewed owls and crushed worms ~

Dodge the doctor

Some people didn't fancy visiting their doctor or dentist – especially the dentist. Yet the dentists were no worse than they are today.

They would invite you to lie on the floor and strap you down. Then they would kneel over you with your head between their legs, say, 'We'll have this out in no time!' and get to work. Just like your dentist, eh? What on earth is there to be afraid of?

If you were really rich then the dentist could have a poor child lying beside you. As soon as your bad tooth was whipped out (or ripped out) a good 'live' tooth would be pulled from the child and planted in the gap in your gums. (Don't worry, the child would be paid!)

Other toothless patients had false teeth made from tusks of hippopotamus or walrus or from pottery. These false teeth never fitted very well and were often taken out so the wearer could eat a meal. (Still they were better than Victorian false teeth made from rubber and celluloid. Sydney Dark fell asleep with a cigar clamped between his celluloid teeth. When the cigar burnt down it set fire to his teeth!)

But let's suppose you were a real wimp and wanted to dodge the doctor and dentist. Here are ten Georgian cures you may like to try. There's just one problem … nine of the

79

crazy cures were actually tried by the Georgians. One has been made up and was never used by the Georgians – or anyone else. Can you spot which is the odd one out…

1 James Woodforde had a sty on his eyelid. He heard that it would go if he rubbed it with the tail of a black cat. He tried it … and it worked!

2 Thomas Grey's friend suffered from swollen joints and heard that boiling a whole chicken and eating it with six litres of beer would cure him. He tried it … and it worked!

3 People bitten by a mad dog could catch the dog's disease, rabies. The cure was to take a hair from the dog and put it on the wound or swallow it … this never worked.

4 Toothache is easily cured. Take a poker and heat it in the fire. When it is nice and hot then burn the ear lobe with the poker and the pain in the tooth will go away.

5 Lavinia Cordle found that a boil on her bottom was painful. Bursting it with a needle caused the boil to spread. Her friend said the trick was to burst it suddenly. Lavinia lifted her skirts and bent over with her back to a horse. Her friend tickled the horse's leg with a stalk of straw. When the kick of the horse landed on Lavinia's backside, the boil burst. The iron of the horse's hoof helped the sore spot to heal in half the time. Lavinia was able to sit down within a month – as soon as the bruise from the kick went away.

NOW HE HAS A SMELLY MOUTH AND SMELLY EARS

6 Bad breath caused by rotten teeth could be a problem. (You can tell if you have bad breath – friends like to chat to you from the far end of a football pitch with a megaphone.) The Georgians believed the best cure was to scrape the skin off a turnip, roast the pieces and wear them behind the ear.

7 Another Georgian cure for rabies was said to be a bath in salt water or, even better, a dunk in the sea. A man from Bristol was bitten and taken out to sea in a boat. He said, 'I'll never survive the dip in the sea!' They dipped him anyway and pulled him back into the boat, where he immediately died.

AT LEAST HE HASN'T GOT RABIES ANY MORE

8 A wasp sting inside the throat can kill you. The Georgians believed that you should swallow the juice of an onion to cure a sting like that. It may save your life. And the wasp will buzz off with its eyes full of tears. (Of course the best cure is not to go around with your mouth open.)

9 An adder sting is nasty ... and the Georgian cure was nastier! In 1821 a woman was bitten by an adder near Southampton and was a long way from a doctor. The local people took a chicken, killed it and placed its warm guts over the wound. Sounds *foul*, but they said it worked.

10 Smallpox had killed many people through the ages but the Georgians found a way of preventing it – vaccination. They actually gave people a cattle sickness called cow pox. The cow pox didn't harm them but it did keep the smallpox sickness away.

Answer: 5. The other crazy cures were all really tired. And number **10**, vaccination, is a brilliant Georgian invention that has led to thousands of modern cures and saved millions of lives.

Bedlam, blood, blisters and baths

If you had problems with your mind it was a dreadful life for you in Georgian times. Mentally ill people were called 'mad' and locked away. Treatments included…

- being beaten
- being thrown into cold baths
- being made to vomit
- having blood let out of the body.

The most famous Georgian to suffer mental illness was King George III. So-called treatments included…

- fastening him to his bed

I NEED TO SCRATCH MY NOSE!

- shouting at him – after stuffing handkerchiefs in the king's mouth so he couldn't answer back

WHY CAN'T I STUFF THE HANDKERCHIEFS IN MY EARS?

- forming blisters on his head then bursting them – to let the badness out of his head

- giving him medicines that made him so sick he prayed to be cured or dead.

George's joke
George's behaviour was strange but he wasn't stupid. He was visited by a new doctor, Doctor Willis, and he hated the man on sight. The king questioned the man...

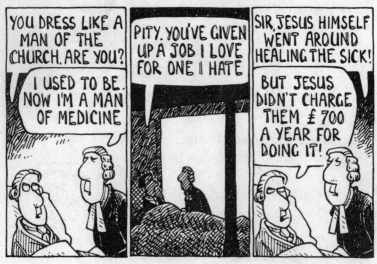

In fact Willis was later paid £10,000 (over half a million pounds at today's value) to treat mad Queen Maria of Portugal. He failed to cure her but was paid anyway.

Still, George could have been treated worse! Ordinary people in London's Bethlehem Hospital (known as Bedlam for short) were chained in their cells if they had mental problems. The porters in charge of the hospital made extra pocket money – they let the public look into the cells to 'give them cause for laughter' and charged a penny.

Gory Georgian fun and games

The people of Georgian Britain liked to enjoy themselves in great crowds. They flocked to fairs and packed into parks, thronged theatres and crowded coffee shops.

Of course Georgians didn't have televisions to amuse them. But maybe you'd swap a night's television for the fun of the Georgian fair? You could see…

• Miller the German Giant (other 'freak shows' included 'a girl of 15 with strange moles on her backside')
• Violante the acrobat
• a conjuror
• a waxworks display
• a fire-eater
• a performing dog
• a dancing horse
• a slack-rope walker (unless he'd had a bit too much to drink, in which case he'd become a 'tight' rope walker). Slack-rope walker Madame Margaretta stood on one leg on a rope and balanced 13 full glasses on a tobacco pipe.

There were one or two horrors you might not enjoy so much, like…

- bear-baiting (the bear was chained to a post. Spectators paid a shilling each to set their dogs on the bear.)
- badger-baiting
- cock fights (often arranged in village churchyards!)
- goose-riding (a goose was hung from a tree by its feet. Riders would gallop underneath it and try to snatch its head off. This was made difficult by greasing the bird's beak.)

Any sort of cruelty to animals was enjoyed by some people. One advert announced…

A *WILD BULL* will be turned loose with *fireworks all over him*

Not quite so bad was cruelty to humans at a fair which advertised…

A player of bagpipes

There were also fights between women. A foreign visitor called Cesar de Sassure described one…

> Both women wore very little clothing. One was a stout Irishwoman and the other a small Englishwoman, full of fire and very nippy. The weapons were a sort of blunt, two-handed sword. Presently the Irishwoman received a cut across the forehead and that put a stop to the first part of the fight. The Englishwoman's supporters threw money and cheered for her. During this time the wounded woman's forehead was sewn up, this being done on stage, she drank a large glass of spirits and the fight began again. The Irishwoman was wounded a second time then a third time with a long and deep wound all across her neck and throat. A few coins were thrown to her but the winner made a good income from the fight.

In another fight two women fought a 'boxing and scratching match' till their faces were covered in blood and their clothes torn off their bodies. It sounds a bit like a girls' hockey match today, only not so violent.

In a London club a man fought three women at the same time and knocked them all out.

De Sassure went on to describe men fighting with the same weapons. The loser's ear was almost cut from his head.

A public notice appeared in Gateshead in County Durham on 22 May 1758. It read…

*On this day
the annual ENTERTAINMENTS
at Swalwell Fair will take place
This will consist of…*

~ Dancing for ribbons
~ Women running for smocks
~ Ass races
~ Foot races for men
~ With the odd whim of a man eating a
  cockerel alive, feathers, entrails and all !!!

In Cambridge in 1770 a 16-year-old boy 'ate a whole cat smothered with onions.' But at least the cat was dead and cooked!

Sports and games you may not want to play

1 Fighting animals Eating a live chicken sounds cruel but cock-fighting was still a popular sport and bull-baiting was watched by huge crowds. In some places it was finally stopped when spectators were injured. The magistrates didn't stop it because they were worried about the cruelty to the animals. Rich people, like the Duke of Cumberland, got pleasure from setting a tiger to kill a stag … in a 1764 contest the stag won.

2 Horse racing Horse racing could be cruel. Horses raced time and again in heats as long as four miles. The exhausted horse that won the most heats was the winner.

There was also cruelty to jockeys – they were fond of barging, pushing and whipping their opponents. A writer said…

I remember one jockey who used to boast of the damage he did by striking with the handle of his whip. He liked to describe the number of eyes and the teeth he had beaten out.

A lot of money was gambled on horse races and some gamblers were bad losers. They sometimes set upon a jockey with sticks and stones and whips!

3 Soccer Football games were often organized in the street. Two sides booted a leather ball filled with air and weren't too bothered about how many windows they broke in houses and coaches. In Gloucester in 1811 the *Shrewsbury Chronicle* reported…

> An apprentice was convicted of playing football on a Sunday. He was sentenced to 14 days in prison.

Nowadays he'd be paid £10,000 a week and sentenced to play 90 minutes a week! (That's about £1.85 a second.)

4 Cricket In 1748 a court finally decided that another dreadfully dangerous game was actually legal – though people had been playing it for hundreds of years. This weird game was called 'cricket.' Teams of men (with some women players in London) threw a hard ball at some wooden pegs. The players wore no pads or gloves so broken bones, torn fingernails and bleeding injuries were common. A farmer was killed by a cricket ball in 1825. Maybe a return to Georgian cricket would liven the sport up today! Or this unusual Surrey match of 1773…

> Last Wednesday an extraordinary match of cricket was played on Guildford Downs between a carpenter on one side and nine tailors on the other side. The prize was a quarter of lamb and a cabbage. The match was won by the Carpenter by 64 runs.

What a pity that Georgian carpenter isn't around to play for England's cricket team today. In 1997 England's cricketers lost to Matabeleland and Zimbabwe – in Britain in 1770 nobody had even heard of Matabeleland and Zimbabwe!

5 Hunting The deer hunting of earlier times went out of fashion and fox-hunting became the most popular entertainment for the upper classes. Hare hunting was popular too because hares didn't run so far.[1] In 1790 a hare actually escaped from the pack and the *Newcastle Chronicle* reported…

> The hare fled and, with a wonderful leap, darted through a pane of glass in a window of The Globe Inn. It landed amongst a pile of legal papers since the inn was crowded with lawyers at the time. As soon as they recovered from the shock, the lawyers presented the poor hare to the cook…

You'd think the lawyers would have given it a fair hare trial, wouldn't you? But that's life. Hare today, gone tomorrow.

6 Rugby In 1823 two teams of boys were playing football at Rugby school when William Webb Ellis picked up the ball and ran with it. This new idea became quite popular (it gives your feet a rest) and the school had invented a new ball game! What should they call it? William-Webb-Ellis-Ball?

1. Popular for ladies and gentlemen, that is. Two boys who killed a hare for food were given a public whipping in Reading in 1773.

No. How about Pick-it-up-and-run-with-it-till-somebody-jumps-on-you-ball? That's better.

STRANGE...
IT SEEMS
TO HAVE
GOT DARK

7 Ballooning In Newcastle Upon Tyne, there was a report of a new entertainment in 1786. An old history book told the story...

Mr Lunardi, the famous aeronaut, made an attempt to ascend in an air balloon from the river bank. In filling it Mr Lunardi added the last of the acid and the hot steam became remarkably strong and thick. This gave so much alarm to those on that side of the balloon, who thought that it was on fire, that they immediately let go of 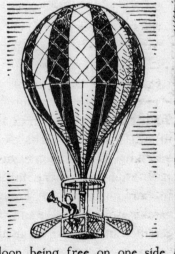 their side of the net. The balloon being free on one side made a sudden stretch upwards. The balloon, set free, ascended rapidly and dragged with it Master Ralph Heron. The boy had one of the balloon ropes twisted round his hand and arm. When he reached a height of 500 feet the rope snapped off the balloon and he fell into a nearby garden. He died soon after.

8 Chuckstones This game involves throwing up stones and catching them on the back of the hand. It's been popular since ancient times but two Georgian boys came up with a new version in 1760. You could call it 'kill-a-wrinkly'…

In a small Devon village an old labouring man, John Wilson, was lying on a bench fast asleep. Some boys were playing at 'chuckers' and the old man's mouth being open, one of them chucked a stone directly into his mouth. This woke him, but the stone stuck in his throat and choked him before help could be brought. The man was over 90 years old and had never had any sickness.

Let that be a lesson to all you chuckstone players. Never, ever sleep with your mouth open.

9 Bull running Put a rather angry bull in a pen at the end of a road, then go off to the local tavern for a few drinks – you'll need them. Come back and open the gate of the bull pen. Then run. If the bull catches you it will toss you on its horns or gore you. This is no fun at all. But if the bull catches someone else and throws them up in the air it is terrific fun. In 1785 a Lincoln newspaper grumbled that it was a stupid and wasteful sport…

10 Pinching matches Two people stand toe to toe and pinch one another. The one who can stand it the longest is the winner. If a player gets angry or starts to swear then he or she is the loser.

IT'S ALL RIGHT SIS', YOU CAN GO FIRST

The *Hertfordshire Mercury* reporter described a contest between a 'puny' little man and a 'stout' man…

They kept pinching each other for an hour, chiefly on the flesh parts of the arm. At the end of that time the stout man's arms fell powerless to his side and he had to give in from exhaustion and pain. The puny man offered to fight any man in England for the pinching championship.

...and games you definitely wouldn't want to play

1 A newspaper report of 1818 described this game that turned into gore...

> On Saturday three boys were playing in a field where some cows were feeding. One of them, about 16 years of age, suggested that they tie another to the tail of a cow. But the enraged animal dragged the victim up and down the field at full speed, plunging in all directions. Before he could be rescued his life was totally extinct.

2 Apple bobbing is popular today but one Georgian invented 'silver bobbing'. A silver coin was dropped into a tub of water and players had to pick it up using their teeth. If you think apple bobbing's hard then don't try this.

3 In 1764 a bored lord in Huntingdon invented a game called 'hunting the hen'. The players had their hands muffled in thick bandages. They had to catch a hen and pull a feather out. The first to take a feather won the hen.

Did you know…?

A man called Jedediah Buxton travelled the country, entertaining people as a mathematical wonder. Jed had never been taught to read or write but he was famous for his maths skills. He was once asked to work out how many hairs' breadths (at 48 hairs to the inch) it would take to reach from Tyneside to London. He answered in less than three minutes (and without a pocket calculator) 833,310,720. And that, give or take a few curls, is about right!

A game you might like to play
A jingling match

This was a popular game played by women at fairs and can be played by a class of pupils in a school hall, yard or field.

You need:

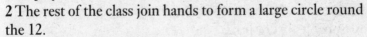

• a bell on a string
• 12 scarves.

To play:

1 12 players are selected.

2 The rest of the class join hands to form a large circle round the 12.

3 One player – the Jingler – has the bell hung round her (or his) neck and her hands tied behind her with a scarf.

4 The other 11 players have scarves tied over their eyes.

5 The blindfolded players try to catch the Jingling player who can move anywhere in the circle to escape.

6 If the Jingler escapes for one minute then he or she wins.

7 If a blindfolded player catches the jingler then he or she wins and becomes the Jingler.

A jingling match

Prizes:
Decided by the players before the game. A new computer or a trip to the Bahamas (paid for by the teacher) would be a reasonable sort of prize.

Wacky Georgian words

The language we use is forever changing. Old words are forgotten or get new meanings and new ones are invented. Georgian Britain was no different.

Forgotten words include *odsbodikins* (a swear word) and *hock-dockies* for shoes. What a sad loss they are.

Changed words included *respectable* to mean polite. (And the Georgians tried to be polite. They used fewer swear words. No *respectable* person said *belly* or *bitch* any longer.)

The bill for food at a tavern was called the *scran*. It changed in Georgian times to mean the food itself … and it still does.

New words came along with new fashions. A man in Georgian times could often be judged by the size of his hair-piece. So what did they call a very important man? A *bigwig* of course.

If you are going to understand the Georgians you probably need to know some of their words.

Match the following words to their meanings…

1. A blue pigeon flier	a. is an idiot
2. A louse trap	b. is a coat
3. A sumph	c. is a horse
4. A wooden suit	d. is a gossip
5. A daisy-kicker	e. is a comb
6. A magpie	f. is a neck
7. A cover-me-queerly	g. is a thief who steals the lead off your roof
8. A sad man	h. is a coffin
9. A tattle box	i. is a trouble-maker
10. A scrag	j. is a small coin

Answers:

1g) *Blue pigeon* is lead, probably because of the colour.

2e) Obvious when you think about it. Similar to the delightful modern phrase 'nit rake'.

3a) That's a Scottish word. You can probably get away with calling your teacher this … unless your teacher is an expert in Scottish words in which case you'll be needing a wooden suit!

4h) So don't let anyone measure you for a wooden suit! (Just say, 'It wooden suit me.')

5 c) So, if your name is Daisy then don't go near a horse.

6j) Also known as a maggie. But watch out for a maggie rab in Scotland because it's a forged coin.

7b) Actually a ragged coat. If you have a good coat then you can call it a *cover-me-decent* … which it will.

8i) Of course if you're a troublemaker who gets caught then you'll be a sad, sad man.

9d) Just like a match box is full of matches, a lunch box is full of lunch, a tattle-box is full of tattle. So why isn't a pillar-box full of pillars?

10f) The Georgian meaning of *scragging* someone is hanging them. So, a scrag boy would hang you from the *scragging-post* till your scrag was totally *scragged*!

Rotten revolutions

Britain has always suffered from riots. The Georgians seemed to suffer more than most.

A writer said…

> *I have seen this year riots in the country about corn; riots about elections; riots about workhouses; riots of miners, riots of weavers, riots of wood-cutters; and I have seen riots of smugglers in which law officers have been murdered and the king's troops fired at.*

And this was in 1769. Twenty years later the French had a terrifying revolution where the king and the nobles were executed. The Georgians feared the same could happen over here. It never did, but the British went to war with the French Emperor who replaced the headless king, Emperor Napoleon Bonaparte.

Napoleon expected the British people to support a revolution – after all, there had been all of those riots. When he sent French soldiers to help a British revolution he got a surprise…

Mum's army

In 1797 a French force of 1,400 soldiers landed on the Welsh coast and they expected the local people to help them. They thought there would be a Welsh Revolution that would drive out the evil English. The defence of Britain rested on Lord Cawdor of Stackpole Hall.

If Lord Cawdor had written to a friend of the time he may have admitted that his victory was a great surprise – to the British defenders more than the French attackers!

February 1797

My dear Thomas,

You have probably heard the tale of the
French invasion of Wales by now. But the truth
is even stranger than the reports that have
appeared in the newspapers. Of course they say
I'm a hero, but to tell the truth I had some
unexpected luck.

I was having supper at Stackpole Hall when
a messenger arrived on a horse that was foaming
with sweat and more dead than alive. 'Lord
Cawdor!' he cried. 'The French have arrived!'

'What? Here? Now?' I asked. 'They're just in
time for supper.'

'No!' he groaned. 'Thousands of them have
landed at Fishguard! They're raiding every
farm in the area. They're stealing every drop
of wine they can find.'

'Anyone been hurt?' I asked.

'Not exactly.' the man shrugged. 'They're a
bit nervous. They're shooting at anything that
moves. Huw Thomas at Pencaer Farm said
one of the French soldiers came into his
parlour and heard a noise behind him. He

turned and fired wildly.'

'Did he hit anyone?'

'No but he wrecked Huw's grandfather clock. That's what was making the noise, you see?'

I couldn't believe what I was hearing, Thomas. 'So, we have a couple of thousand scared Frenchmen shooting our clocks. And you've ridden 30 miles to tell me this? It's Colonel Knox you should be telling. He's the man in charge of the local defence force, the Fishguard Fencibles.'

'Colonel Knox was at a ball when he got the news. He said "The Fishguard Fencibles are no match for a French army." He decided to retreat.'

I can tell you, Thomas. I almost exploded with rage. 'He ran away!'

'He retreated, sir.' the miserable messenger said.

'Then the Stackpole Yeomanry will have to show him how its done.' I said.

I guess it took less than an hour for the men to come in from the surrounding villages, gather their weapons and meet at Stackpole Hall. Of course everyone had heard about the invasion and my men were ready for them. We set off for Haverfordwest the next morning, camped there and gathered more men, then set off for Fishguard the day after. I suppose we had 500 men in all by the time we spotted the French camp.

Now my men were spoiling for a fight, but it was clear the French outnumbered us. So I sent a message to their commander. 'My forces are growing stronger every hour. Surrender now or you will be wiped out.' It was a lie, of course, but the commander's reply was the last thing I expected.

The French commander was actually one of those rebel American fellows. A man called William Tate. His reply said: 'We surrender on condition that the men you have already captured are set free.'

I accepted his surrender and met him at Fishguard harbour to take his men's weapons and accept the surrender. And that's when I told him, 'We haven't actually captured any of your men.'

The American shook his head and pointed up the main street. 'Your British Army red-coats took 20 of our men. The rest of the French were so drunk they ran away when the red-coats attacked.'

Now I knew that the nearest red-coat army was still 40 miles away in Carmarthen. But when I looked along the harbour I saw 20 French soldiers trooping along looking very sorry for themselves. And they weren't being held by red-coats... they were being marched along by red cloaks! A little group of women were wearing their red Welsh cloaks and those tall black hats they have in this country. They were armed with pitch-forks and reaping hooks and they had the French terrified.

The woman in charge strode across to me. A huge woman – she certainly terrified me. She threw a huge salute and grinned. 'Mistress Jemima Nicholas at your service,' she said.

It seems the French had made the mistake of trying to attack these women and they'd been taken prisoner instead. The rest of the

French invaders had lost heart and persuaded Tate to surrender.

So there you have it! They say the Stackpole Yeomanry and I are the heroes. The truth is the mighty Jemima Nicholas and the women of Fishguard have saved our country from the invaders. Her name should go down in history with heroines like Boudicca and Queen Elizabeth.

God save the King, and God bless you too my friend.   yours   Robert Lord Cawdor

Everybody remembers the first French invasion – they remember King Harold the hero who died with an arrow in his eye. But he was a man and a king so he's remembered even though he lost.

Sadly Jemima Nicholas and the Pembroke 'Mum's Army' have been almost forgotten. She was a woman, of course, and it doesn't seem to matter that she actually won! (You could be reading this in French if she hadn't!)

After this defeat the French never tried invading Britain again. In fact no invader has landed on Britain's shores since. (Unless you count a few German pilots shot down in World War II.)

During the Napoleonic Wars Lord Nelson and the navy protected the British from attack by sea. Then British armies crossed to the continent and finally defeated the French at the Battle of Waterloo in 1815.

A few troublemakers tried to copy the French Revolution in Britain, but they didn't get much support. George III kept his head.

The American Revolution

Of course the British had another Revolution to worry about. They had some colonies on the far side of the Atlantic Ocean in a place called America. It had been a good place to dump convicts at one time.

But in the reign of George III those American Colonists started to get stroppy. They weren't happy with being told what to do by a king and a parliament back in Britain. They wanted to make their own decisions – they wanted to be free to kill Native Americans and steal their land, free to invent hamburgers and free to play cowboys. But above all, they wanted to be free of paying tax to Britain.

Not everybody in America wanted to be a rebel, of course. But the Americans who tried to stay loyal to Britain could be given a tough time.

The diary of a rebel tells what happened to one American soldier who disagreed with his rebel friends...

> 8 August 1775.
> Riflemen took a man in New Milford who had called them 'damned rebels' and other insulting names. They made him walk

> in front of them to Litchfield, a journey
> of 20 miles. He was made to carry one
> of his geese in his hand all the way. When
> they arrived there they covered him in
> tar and made him pluck his goose. They
> stuck the feathers to him, drummed him out
> of the rifle company, forced him to kneel
> down and thank them for being so
> merciful to him.

(The writer of the diary doesn't say what happened to the goose, but they probably cut it up, covered it in batter and fried it – another American invention: *Litchfield Fried Goose*, perhaps?)

In the end America got the freedom they wanted. Britain couldn't fight a war at a distance of 3,000 miles. They created a new country – the United States of America – and elected a president instead of a king. They picked a leading rebel fighter, George Washington, to be the first President.

Back in Britain poor old George III was the loser – he lost the American Colonies and went on to lose his marbles.

The Luddite revolts

The Industrial Revolution meant that one man and a machine could do the work of (maybe) ten men. It meant that nine men were put out of work. They were not a happy nine men. Some of the nine believed that the answer was to smash up the machine!

(This does not make a lot of sense. One horse could do the work of ten men – pulling a plough, say – but you didn't see farm workers going around beating up horses, did you?)

Trouble started in 1811 in Yorkshire and spread through Nottinghamshire and Lancashire. Machine breakers gathered in gangs and marched like an army to destroy machines. The army was called in to defend the machines with guns – the machine-wreckers armed themselves with guns. Many died in the battles that followed.

Machine owners who tried to defend themselves were murdered – the murderers were hanged – the youngest to hang was a boy of 15 and the oldest a man of nearly 70.

These machine smashers were called Luddites because they were said to follow the mighty machine-breaker, Ned Ludd. 'Disobey Ned Ludd and you die!'

The very name brought fear to the hearts of the mill-owners, mothers used the name to scare their children: 'Behave yourself or Ned Ludd will get you!'

But who was this Ned Ludd? The truth is he was never a rebel leader. This is what happened...

The truth is the Luddites never had any leader. Each group was dealt with by the army one at a time and the Luddite riots died as quickly as they had started.

If they'd had a single, strong leader it might have been different, but they never had one. They certainly never had one called Ned Ludd – and Ned Ludd was never a Luddite.

The Peterloo massacre

The machine wreckers went quiet for a long time while the war against Napoleon came to its bloody end at the Battle of Waterloo in 1815.

But soldiers came home to a Britain where corn prices were getting higher and wages were getting lower. When that happens, of course, you get hungry … and you get angry.

By 1819 the people of the north were particularly angry.

A huge meeting was called at Saint Peter's Fields near Manchester. Workers and their families came from all over the north to hear the famous Henry Hunt speak about the changes the workers wanted. Above all they wanted to vote for members of parliament.

Sixty thousand people packed into the fields till, someone said, 'their hats were almost touching.'

But the magistrates of the area panicked. They called in soldiers to keep the crowds in order. But, in the front line, were the part-time soldiers – local men who were not very well trained but enjoyed wearing the uniforms and swaggering around. Their regiment was called The Manchester and Salford Yeomanry Cavalry – the MYC for short.

In France the angry people turned against the nobles. But in Britain they turned against each other. That was the difference.

Workers didn't like the Prince of Wales who ruled the country while his father was mentally ill. But they really, really hated men like Tom Shelmerdine … one of their own people who tried to stop their peaceful protest.

If Tom Shelmerdine had kept a diary then it may have looked like this. The diary is imaginary, only the sad facts are true…

Tom Shelmerdine's diary

Workers gathering into a union to get higher wages was against the law in 1819. Many workers wanted to change the law but they couldn't gather together to protest against because it was against the law to gather together and protest!

Some tried. But Tom Shelmerdine of Manchester wasn't one of them…

> *21 May 1819 Some of the men in the weaving mill are traitors. I'm sure they're planning to form one of those trade union things. Of course they don't tell me. They think I'll report them and have them arrested. They're right. I would.*

For the workers who didn't want to join a union there was something else they could do…

> *27 May 1819 I'll join the loyal subjects of King George and put a stop to the mill-workers' treason*

> I'll join the yeomanry. They train in their spare time and it's a little extra pay. But best of all they are standing up to the troublemakers.

The local guard regiments were amateurs. A bit like boy scouts with big swords…

> 9 June 1819 Joined the MYC. I look very smart in the uniform though I say it myself. A nice blue with white trim. Yes, very smart. Of course I'm not very good on a horse, but none of the other lads of the MYC are either.

In the summer of 1819 the workers of the north planned a peaceful protest. The leaders taught the protesters how to march in formation. They wanted this protest to look really well organized – not just a mob. But the magistrates and the law officers got the wrong idea entirely…

> 27 June 1819 The weavers have started marching. They are practising drill like an army. The MYC lads reckon they are planning an attack. The yeomanry send their swords away to be polished every month. But this time they've sent them to be sharpened. I keep falling off my brute of a horse.

A meeting planned for 60,000 people couldn't be kept a secret from the magistrates for long, of course…

> 13 July 1819 Major Trafford, our commander, has told us the rebel secret. They are planning a meeting. The trouble-maker Henry Hunt will

> be at this meeting and he'll be stirring them up.
> The lads of the MYC will be there as well, we hope,
> with our sharpened swords. Harry Bardon cut
> himself at last night's practice.

On the morning of 16 August 1819 the workers gathered all over the north and began marching to St Peter's Fields for the great meeting. Meanwhile the full time soldiers, the Hussars, gathered in Manchester. The part-time soldiers, the MYC, gathered in the local pubs! Giving big swords to boy scouts is not a good idea. Giving big swords and strong drink to boy scouts is stupid. But that's what Hugh Hornby Birley did with the MYC…

> 16 August 1819 Sixty thousand traitors in
> St Peter's Fields, they reckon. The MYC are in
> this public house and ready. Mr Hugh Hornby
> Birley is buying us as much ale as we want.
> They say the rebels in St Peter's Fields are
> quiet and orderly. But we think that's just a
> trick. When the signal comes we'll be ready. Here
> it is now! The constables are going to arrest
> Henry Hunt! And the MYC, not the hussars,
> have been chosen to escort them.
> To horse Lads!

Of course a lot of the drunken MYC had trouble climbing on their horses, never mind staying on them. The crowds were packed into the field. The constables struggled to get through to Hunt on the platform. So the gallant MYC drew their sabres and hacked their way through. The rest is horrible history…

17 August 1819 It's over. It was exciting, I think, but I don't remember too much about it. I do remember we galloped onto the field and you should have seen those traitors panic! They'd have run away if they hadn't been so crowded together. They started to scream and that was a big mistake. Well, I mean, it panicked the horses and they went wild. Some of us have enough trouble with a quiet horse. Imagine how dangerous we were on scared horses. I came face to face with old Meg Willis. She recognised me, of course, because she used to nurse me as a child. 'Nay Tom Shelmerdine, thee will not hurt me, I know!' she said. Of course I wouldn't. But the horse did, the brutish animal. Still, it has to be said, if old Meg hadn't been there then she wouldn't have been killed.

Tom Shelmerdine was remembered, and hated, because of the way he rode down the old woman who used to nurse him. Other MYC riders struck out wildly with their sharp sabres. They cut their way through the crowds to get to Hunt. It was a bit like boy scouts cutting their way through a tangled wood – but it wasn't bushes they were hacking at – they were human beings.

18 August 1819 There's a lot of bad feeling about that St. Peter's Fields business. The newspapers are mocking us for charging at unarmed men, women and children. But we

didn't know they were unarmed, did we? They
could have been hiding pikes under their coats
couldn't they? Heroes of Peterloo they are calling
us. They forget, we were only doing our job.

It was the magistrates who sent in the half-trained, half-baked, half-witted MYC when they could have sent in the Hussars. The Hussars went in later and struck people with the flat of their swords to drive them back. The MYC had used the edge of their swords to kill and wound. It's the MYC who were remembered and hated – the local men. These rebels didn't blame the government so much as the French had. They blamed the people they knew. People like Tom Shelmerdine.

So 'Peterloo' killed 11 people and wounded 500.

Peterloo foul facts

- The MYC were sent in to protect the police. But several police were trampled by the rampaging yeomanry. Special Constable Thomas Ashworth died.
- One of the men at the meeting had taken a cheese for his dinner. He stored it under his hat. It saved his life when a sabre chopped at his head!

117

- A weaver called John Lees had lived through the horror of the Battle of Waterloo and Napoleon's powerful army. But at Peterloo he was cut by a sabre, smashed by a truncheon and trampled by a horse. He died.

- The youngest victim was William Fildes, a baby in his mother's arms. She was walking along the street when the MYC galloped, out of control, towards St Peter's Fields. The baby was knocked to the ground and trampled. Mrs Fildes wasn't even at the meeting.
- A poet at the meeting described the charge through the crowd: 'Sabres were used to hew a way through held-up hands and defenceless heads; chopped limbs and wound-gaping skulls were seen; groans and cries were mingled with the din of that horrid confusion.'

- Hunt was arrested and taken to Lancaster Jail. On his return from Lancaster his horse, Bob, died near Preston. He was buried under a weeping willow with a headstone that read, 'Alas! Poor Bob!!!' Thousands of people went to the funeral.

- BUT … seven years later Bob's remains were dug up and his bones turned into snuff boxes. A knee-cap was given a silver lid and presented to Hunt.

Instant 'Peterloo' quiz
The government had an enquiry into the massacre. Who got the blame…
a) The magistrates for sending in the MYC
b) The MYC commanders for getting the men drunk
c) The MYC members for being out of control
d) Henry Hunt for arranging the meeting

Answer: **d)** Of course. What did you expect?

Test your teacher

Teachers love asking questions. They even get paid for it! It would be really boring if every pupil got every question right, so teachers learn to enjoy it when their pupils get the *wrong* answers. Now it's your chance to get your revenge. Test your teacher (or pester your parent) with this amazingly difficult quiz.

When they get a wrong answer you can mutter, 'I thought you'd have known that!'

1 What would a Georgian doctor do with a 'pelican'?
a) Train it to catch fish alive so patients could swallow them and cure swamp fever.
b) Use it to pull out a deeply rooted, rotten tooth.
c) Boil its eggs, grind them up with beetroot and make plague plasters.

2 In 1750 a gentleman bought a pound of tea from a smuggler. He didn't like the look of the tea so he fed it to the dog. What happened next?
a) The dog became a tea addict and had to be fed a saucer every day.

DOG AND BONE CHINA

DOG AND BONE

b) The dog refused to drink it until the gentleman added sugar and milk.

HOW MANY TIMES HAVE I GOT TO TELL YOU, MILK FIRST, *THEN* THE TEA!

c) The dog had a fit and died.

3 What did Robinson Cruso do for a living?
a) He made beds and auctioned furniture.
b) He was a sailor who enjoyed being shipwrecked and writing about it.
c) He was a writer whose most famous book was about a desert island.

4 Carlisle Spedding invented a steel mill – it struck sparks off a flint stone and gave light. Useful for pitmen in a coal mine. But … when it was used in a mine it could explode firedamp gas. It killed a lot of miners. But how did Spedding himself die?
a) His steel mill set fire to his wig.
b) His steel mill failed, he stumbled in the dark and fell in a river.
c) His steel mill caused an explosion of firedamp in a coal mine and killed him.

5 A gentleman in Georgian Britain would not wear what?
a) Trousers.
b) A waistcoat.
c) Stockings.

6 Tearing hares apart with hounds is an ancient sport, enjoyed by the Georgians. But when was it stopped?
a) Not until 1826 in the reign of George IV.
b) Not until 1897 in the reign of Queen Victoria.
c) Not at all. Hare hunting is still legal in Britain.

7 The Georgians spent a lot of time at war with France. They weren't too keen on any foreigners. What did they do to some foreigners on the streets of London?
a) Spat at them.

b) Threw dead cats and dogs at them.

c) Swore at them in French.

8 Sailors in Nelson's navy suffered bad food. The cheese was often too hard to eat, but they had another use for that. What?
a) They used it in mouse traps. The mice broke their teeth on the cheese and starved.

b) The sailors carved the cheese with their knives to make tough, hard wearing buttons for their coats.
c) They used the cheeses to play a game like shove-ha'penny on deck. It was called shove cheddar.

9 What useful thing did the watchmaker Andrew Cumming invent in 1775 that we still use today?
a) A stink trap.
b) Roller skates.
c) Knickers held up with elastic.

10 Highwaymen couldn't always afford pistols. In 1774 a Huntingdon highwayman held up a coach using what?
a) A bow and arrow.

b) A savage dog.

c) A candlestick.

Answers:

1b) A 'pelican' was a tool for pulling out difficult teeth. When pliers failed to remove the tooth, the pelican would rip it out sideways.

A careless doctor could rip out good teeth along with the bad. There were even cases of good teeth being torn out and the bad one left! The instrument got its name because it looked like a pelican's beak.

A pelican with some bad teeth

2c) The dog died and the gentleman complained to the local newspaper. Of course the gentleman couldn't complain to the law because he should not have been buying cheap tea from a smuggler. He couldn't complain to the smuggler because no one could trace him. Still, he was lucky. If he'd drunk the tea he wouldn't have complained to anybody – ever again!

3a) Robinson Cruso, a bed-maker, lived in Kings Lynn High Street. The writer Daniel Defoe visited Kings Lynn on his travels and must have seen the name Robinson Cruso outside the shop. Defoe then told the story of shipwrecked sailor Alexander Selkirk and changed his name … to Robeson Cruso. (Later publishers changed the spelling to Robinson Crusoe.) So, next time your parents tell you to 'make your bed' say, 'Who do you think I am? Robinson Crusoe?' That'll confuse them!

STRANGE CHILD

MAYBE IT'S TOO MUCH READING

4c) Carlisle Spedding's invention caused an explosion. Poor old Spedding. Spark – boom! – and Spedding is speeding up a mine-shaft!

5a) Peasants wore trousers to work in the fields and a gentleman would not be so common as to wear them. Gentlemen wore tighter fitting 'breeches' with stockings. Did you guess that? If not it was a turn-up for the books!

6c) That's right. Hare 'coursing' as it's called is still enjoyed today by many people and many packs of hounds. The hares must enjoy it too, otherwise they'd arm themselves with hare-rifles, wouldn't they?

IF THEIR DOG GOT TORN UP, WOULD THEY STILL ENJOY IT?

7b) It makes you wonder where they got the dead cats and dogs from! Were they just lying around in the street for ruffians to pick up and throw when they saw a foreigner? Or did they say, 'Look! A foreigner. Let's kill a cat and throw it! Here pussy, pussy, pussy!'

8b) The biscuits were worse than the cheese. They were full of black-headed maggots. The sailors usually shut their eyes and ate them. I wonder if the maggots shut their eyes as they were about to be eaten?

MY BISCUIT IS WINKING AT ME

9a) A 'stink trap' is a bend in the toilet pipe that stops smells coming up from the drains. Every home should have one. It's a pity no one's invented a stink trap for a team of boys who have been playing football. Phew!

10c) The candlestick may have looked like the barrel of a pistol but the guard on the coach wasn't fooled. He shot the highwayman with a blunderbuss gun and two slugs ended up in the thief's forehead. The candlestick robber was snuffed out. He probably got on the guard's wick.

Epilogue

George I could have travelled through his new kingdom, Britain, in 1714. He'd have bounced along rutted roads and moved very slowly. From his carriage he'd have seen lots of large areas of common ground divided into strips where poor people farmed their own little piece of land. He'd have seen some magnificent houses and some that were not fit for animals.

SCHÖNE AUSSICHT – SCHADE DASS DIE ARMEN LEUTE IM WEG SIND*

* NICE VIEW, SHAME ABOUT THE POOR

If his great-great-grandson George IV had made the same journey over a hundred years later he may have taken one of the new steam trains – they were sooty and noisy and cold but at least they were much faster. And they'd have crossed over those new canal things. The common ground would be mostly gone and there would be fields closed in with hedges and fences now. The poor people who used to live off the common ground would have gone too. Some would have had to go and work for one of the farmers who owned the fields. More would have gone to the towns.

That would be the biggest change. The towns had become huge and crowded; factory smoke blackened the skies and faces of the workers. The factories made Georgian Britain the richest nation on Earth ... and made some lucky people very rich too. The Georgians also left behind a world that was famous for its slums and some unfortunate people who had to live and die in them.

The gorgeous Georgians changed some things for the better – they got rid of slave trading in their country and they avoided the worst horrors of revolutions.

But would *you* like to have lived in Georgian Britain? If you have money, and if you like to make yourself look gorgeous with make-up and wigs and fine clothes, then you might have enjoyed it!

But Georgian Britain is a bit like the moon; it's bright and flashy to look at from a distance … you may even like to visit it … but you wouldn't want to live there.
Would you?

GORGEOUS
GEORGIANS

GRISLY QUIZ

**Now find out if you're a
Gorgeous Georgians expert!**

QUICK GEORGIAN QUESTIONS

This was the age when pirates were the scourge of the seas, highwaymen haunted the roads, a crackpot was king and the Americans were revolting ... some things never change. It was also the age of thick make-up, beauty spots, monstrous wigs and padded bosoms – and that was just the men.

1. In 1700 John Asgill went to prison for writing a short book called, A man can go from here to heaven without... Without what? (Clue: everybody does it)

2. In Scotland in 1700 a teacher was whipped through the streets of Edinburgh (don't laugh!). What was his crime? (Clue: tough teacher)

3. In 1707 the son of the Duke of Queensberry murdered a kitchen boy. How did he dispose of the evidence? (Clue: it's in really bad taste)

4. Why did Queen Anne's doctors shave her head and cover her feet in garlic? (Clue: sick idea)

5. Queen Anne died in 1714 and she was buried in a coffin that is almost square. Why? (Clue: if the coffin fits, wear it)

6. German George I took the throne. But where was his wife Dorothea? (Clue: she flirted once too often)

7. In Banff in 1714 the town hangman had to catch stray dogs. He was paid for each dog he caught. How did he prove he'd caught a dog? (Clue: hide!)

8. In 1717 a Scottish teacher murdered two pupils in his charge. Before he was hanged he had an odd punishment. What was it? (Clue: he'd never write on a blackboard again)

9. In 1718 the dreaded pirate Blackbeard was shot and beheaded by a navy officer. Blackbeard's body was thrown over the side of the ship. What's supposed to have happened next? (Clue: maybe he crawled)

10. Many Georgian pirates wore gold earrings. Why? (Clue: go to see?)

11. In 1722 an elephant died on its way to Dundee. What did Doctor Patrick Blair do with the corpse? (Clue: jumbo scientist)

12. In 1724 murderer Maggie Dickson escaped execution. The law said she couldn't be hanged. Why? (Clue: second time lucky)

13. In 1727 George I's hated wife, Dorothea, died. He set off for the funeral but failed to get there. Why? (Clue: a second funeral delayed him)

14. Soon after George I died a raven flew in at the window of his girlfriend, the Duchess of Kendal. She looked after it better than any pet. Why? (Clue: it was something George had crowed about)

15. How can a hot poker cure toothache? (Clue: ear we go again)

16. In 1739 the famous highwayman, Dick Turpin, was

executed. His handwriting was recognized by someone who knew him at school and he was betrayed. Who betrayed Turpin? (Clue: master of treachery)

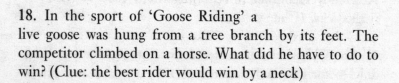

17. George II and his family ate Sunday dinner in style. What could the public buy on those Sundays? (Clue: feeding time at the zoo?)

18. In the sport of 'Goose Riding' a live goose was hung from a tree branch by its feet. The competitor climbed on a horse. What did he have to do to win? (Clue: the best rider would win by a neck)

19. In 1743 George II became the last British monarch to lead an army into battle at Dettingen, Germany. But his horse disgraced him. How? (Clue: might have made a good race horse)

20. In 1746 James Reid played his bagpipes in York. He never played them again. Why not? (Clue: the noise he made was criminal)

21. In 1747 Lord Lovat became the last person to be beheaded in the Tower of London. As he went to his death 20 other innocent people died. How? (Clue: curiosity killed the cat)

FOUL FOR FEMALES

What was it like for Georgian women? Try this simple test – answer true or false...

1. Georgian women put cork balls in their cheeks to improve their appearance.
2. The average age for women to get married was 15.
3. A woman could be burned alive for murdering her husband.
4. Georgian wives were sometimes sold by their husbands at auction.
5. Men were allowed to beat their wives with sticks.
6. Ladies used cement as make-up.
7. The average wage for a maid was £3 a month.
8. Georgian women often took snuff.
9. A group of Welsh women stopped an invasion by the French.
10. It was fashionable for women to have a sun tan.

WACKY WORDS

Can you match the following Georgian words to their meanings...?

1. grunter	a)	idiot
2. hock-docky	b)	hangman's noose
3. sumph	c)	police constable
4. scrag	d)	horse
5. bolly dog	e)	shoe
6. big bug	f)	eye
7. squeezer	g)	shilling coin
8. sad man	h)	neck
9. daisy-kicker	i)	trouble-maker
10. killer	j)	important man

Quick Georgian Questions

1. Dying. The booklet was burned, so we'll never know how to do this clever trick!

2. He had flogged a pupil until the pupil died. And there are still people today who want to bring back beatings for children. Avoid them.

3. He roasted the boy and ate him. Do not try this with your school dinner ladies, please.

4. They were trying to cure her illness. They also blistered her skin with hot irons and gave her medicines to make her vomit. She died – and was probably glad to go.

5. Anne was so fat she was almost square.

6. She was locked away back in Germany. This was her punishment for flirting with Count Konigsmark. It was worse for the count. He'd been murdered and secretly buried at the castle. Jolly George.

7. He collected the skins of the dogs. He was probably happy to do this because one of his other jobs was to sweep up doggy poo from the streets!

8. He had both hands chopped off.

9. It's said Blackbeard's headless corpse swam round the ship three times before finally sinking!

10. They believed it helped their eyesight.

11. He cut it open to see how an elephant's body works.

12. Because she had been hanged once and pronounced dead. As she was taken off to the graveyard in her coffin she sat up! Lucky Maggie lived another 30 years before dying a second time – for good.

13. George died on his way to the funeral. He had held up Dorothea's funeral for six months. If he'd been quicker he'd have had the pleasure of seeing her put six feet under.

14. George had said that he would visit her after his death. She believed the raven was George. Caw! Imagine that!

15. Burning a hole through the lobe of your ear was supposed to cure the pain in the tooth. Crazy! If you ever see your dentist with a hot poker you know it's time to change dentists.

16. Turpin's school master betrayed him.

17. The public could buy tickets to watch George II and the royal family dine. You could try selling tickets for your neighbours to watch you eat your beans on toast!

18. Grab the head of the goose and tear it off. This was made harder by greasing the goose's beak.

19. As soon as it heard enemy gunfire it ran away. George couldn't stop it! The fat little feller had to go back to his command on foot.

20. He was hanged. The bagpipes were declared 'an instrument of war' after the Scottish Jacobite rebellion of 1745. Happily it is now legal to play these beautiful melodic instruments.

21. Spectators crowded on to wooden stands to watch Lovat get lopped. The stands collapsed and killed 20 people. Served them right.

Foul For Females

1. True.

2. False. The average age was about 24. Very few married under 16.

3. True. But this law was changed in 1789 and the punishment was changed to hanging.

4. True. It wasn't legal but it sometimes happened – and continued to happen until 1887.

5. True. But the stick he used had to be no thicker than his thumb, so that's all right.

6. False. But they did use lead paint, arsenic powder and

137

plaster of Paris.

7. False. They would be paid about £3 a year.

8. True.

9. True. In 1797 a small group of women from Pembrokeshire, led by Jemima Nicholas, captured 20 men from the invading French. They were so terrifying that the French army surrendered.

10. False. A pale skin was beautiful to the Georgians and women would sometimes wear a mask in front of the face to protect the skin.

Wacky Words

1.g) 2.e) 3.a) 4.h) 5.c) 6.j) 7.b) 8.i) 9.d) 10.f)

INTERESTING INDEX

Where will you find 'pinching competitions', 'squashed fish eyes' and 'stink traps' in an index? In a Horrible Histories book, of course!

Aborigines (native Australians) 9
American colonies 9, 26, 108–9
animals, cruelty to 86–7, 89, 96, 122, 125
Anne (British queen) 9, 37
Austerlitz, battle of 42

ballooning 93–4
bank notes, forging 53
Blackbeard (British pirate) 59–60
Blair, Tony (British prime minister) 40
bodysnatchers 68–77
boils, on bottom 81
Bow Street Runners (police force) 9
Brummel, Beau (fashion guru) 21

caves
  bones in 54
  living in 32, 58
Charlie (Bonnie Scottish Prince) 9

Cook, Captain (British sea captain) 9
Cresswell, Nicholas (British writer) 35
cricket, legalized 91
cures, crazy 78–85

Defoe, Daniel (British author) 28, 30–32, 34, 124
doctors
  cutting up bodies 78
  dodging 79–82, 84, 120
  selling bodies to 75
dresses, wide 15, 17

Enclosure (fencing off of common land) 30–33

factories, foul 10, 31, 128
fairs 86–7, 97
fans 16–17
fashion
  heights of 16–18

makeovers 12-16
fish eyes, squashed 78
football 91, 126
fops (posers) 18-19
fritters, strawberry 27

gamblers 91
games, gory 86-98
Garrick (British theatre director) 16
George I (British king) 9, 38, 40, 127
George II (British king) 9
George III (British king) 7, 9, 11-12, 35, 41-42, 83, 107-8
George IV (British king) 11, 21, 127
Godfrey's cordial (drugged drink) 45-6

hair, big 14-15, 17
hanging
  in cages 54
  public 64
  reasons for 43, 46, 53, 65-6
  slang for 100
hats
  eaten by cow 18
  fainting at sight of 20
  storing cheese under 117
highwaymen (muggers on horseback) 56-7, 123, 126
Hogarth, William (British cartoonist) 12
Hunt, Henry (British worker's leader) 112, 114-16, 118-19

Industrial Revolution 109

James III (king of Scotland) 9
jingling matches 97-8

Kipling, Rudyard (British poet/writer) 55

lice
  in milk 29
  racing 19
Louis XVI (French king) 10
Luddites (machine smashers) 11, 109-11

Macaronis (fashionable men) 21
MacGregor, Rob Roy (Scottish outlaw) 58
Magna Carta (rights charter) 37
make-up
  men's 21
  poison in 51
  women's 13
Manchester and Salford Yeomanry Cavalry (MYC - part-time soldiers) 112-19
Mum's army (Welsh home guard) 102-7

Napoleon (French emperor) 11, 42, 47, 102, 111, 118
Napoleonic Wars 10, 107
Nelson, Horatio (British sea lord) 10, 107, 122
Nicholas, Jemima (Welsh heroine) 106-7
North, Lord (British prime minister) 41-42

orphans 45-6

Parliament, powerful 36-43, 112
parties, political 37-40
peasants 30-33, 125
Perceval, Spencer (British prime minister) 43
Peterloo massacre 111-19
pets, in prison 66
pinching championships 95
pirates 59-64
Pitt, William the Elder (British prime minister) 41
Pitt, William the Younger (British prime minister) 19, 42-3

Pope, Alexander (British poet/satirist) 12
protests, peaceful 113–14
Puffers (steam trains) 10
punishments, painful 64–7

rebellions/revolutions
    American colonies 9, 108–9
    French peasants 10, 102
    Jacobites 9
    pupils 46–7
rugby 92–3

sandwiches 24
school, surviving 46
Selkirk, Alexander (marooned British sailor)
61, 124
sheep-stealing 66
slave trade 11, 35,60, 128
Smollet, Tobias (British doctor/writer) 28–9
smugglers 55–6, 68, 102, 120, 124
spinners (mill workers) 10, 34
steam power 10–11
Stevenson, Robert Louis (Scottish writer) 62
stink traps 126
Swift, Jonathan (British writer/satirist) 28–9

taxes
    freedom from 108
    on hair powder 19
    on windows 42–3
tea 23, 25, 120, 124
teeth
    from corpses 8
    false 8, 14, 26, 79
    pulling out 120, 124
    rotten 17, 81
toast, invented 23
Tories (political party members) 37–8
Trafalgar, Battle of 10

Trevithick, Richard (British inventor) 10
Turpin, Dick (British highwayman) 56–7

umbrellas 20
unions 113

vaccinations, invented 82
Victoria (British queen) 11

Walpole, Robert (British prime minister) 36,
40–41
Washington, George (American president)
26, 109
Waterloo, Battle of 7-8, 11, 107, 111, 118
Whigs (political party members) 37–8
wigs 14–15, 18–19, 99, 128
William IV (British king) 11
witchcraft, testing for 67
words, wacky 99–101
workhouses, woeful 33, 102

Yorkshire pudding, invented 23

VILE
VICTORIANS

Introduction

History can be horrible! Sometimes you can have horribly clever teachers using horribly funny words…

But you may find that history can be horribly exciting. Stories of great and gory deeds. Even a teacher can get carried away by stirring tales of daring deeds performed by our ancestors…

And sometimes history can be horribly horrible. Some of the things that happened to people may seem horribly disgusting to us…

That's the sort of history you'll find here. Be warned! This book is not for the squeamish. If you have a weak stomach then don't read it – or, if you have to read it, then read it with your eyes closed.

You wouldn't believe some of the things the vile Victorians got up to. After you've read this book you still might not believe them. But they are true, I'm afraid. Some Victorians could be Vicious and Violent and Villainous – Vile, in fact.

When you've finished the book you'll probably know more fascinating facts about the Victorians than your teacher. You may find that History is absolutely Horrible – but learning about it is horribly fascinating.

Be warned, again! This book is not suitable for adults. Victorian adults did some pretty nasty things to children. You wouldn't want your parents or teachers to get any horrible ideas, would you?

Vile Victorians timeline

The good
1837 Victoria becomes queen at the age of 18.
1838 Northumberland girl, Grace Darling, rescues five survivors of a shipwreck.
1830s William Henry Fox Talbot prints his first photographs.

1840 World's first sticky postage stamp – the Penny Black – goes on sale.
1842 Law passed to ban women and children from working in mines.
1851 The Great Exhibition (of British industry) opens in the Crystal Palace.

1852 The first men's flushing public toilet opens in London– that's a relief!
1867 Joseph Lister, surgeon, uses a disinfectant, Phenol; deaths after surgery fall from 45 per cent to just 15 per cent.
1868 Wilkie Collins writes the first 'detective' story, *The Moonstone*.

1871 Queen Vic opens the Albert Hall, named after her husband— Albert, that is, not Hall!

1877 Mr Boot opens a chemist's shop … and another. (So we have the first pair of Boots.)

1883 First electric railway – a shocking success.

1887 First Sherlock Holmes story published – the case called *A Study in Scarlet*.

1896 First moving pictures seen in public in Britain - films including *The Boxing Kangaroo, Three Skirt Dancers* and *The Epsom Derby* were shown in London.

1901 A non-league club wins the FA Cup. They call themselves Tottenham Hotspur.

The bad

1842 A report reveals that half of all children die before their fifth birthday.

1845 Famine in Ireland as the potato crop fails.

1851 The first cigarettes are sold in Britain - people have been dying for a smoke ever since.

1853 Small earthquake shakes the south of the country.

1854 British troops fight Russian in the Crimea – Florrie Nightingale patches them up.

1858 Telegraph cable laid from Britain to America – it snaps 28 days later!

1861 Prince Albert dies. Victoria goes into mourning … and stays there for the rest of her life!

1870 Charles Dickens dies, 'exhausted by fame' – but filthy rich.

1882 England Cricketers lose to Australia at the Oval for the first time! National disaster! British pride burnt to Ashes!

1883 *Treasure Island* written by Stevenson. 'A story for boys –women are excluded,' he says. Typical.

1890 The first comic, *Comic Cuts*, is printed. As a man dodges a dart he cries, 'That was an arrow escape!' (Groan!)

1891 Education **FREE** for every child – now there's **no** excuse for not going to school.

1896 Speed Limit for cars increased 400 per cent – from 4 mph to 20 mph! Men with red flags out of a job!

1897 George Smith, London Taxi driver, is the first drunken driver ever.

1901 Queen Vic dies aged 81.

The ugly

1837 Robert Cocking jumps 180 metres from a balloon to test a parachute. It doesn't work. Splatt!

1846 Report says over 40,000 people are living in cramped cellars in Liverpool.

1849 Two thousand people a week die in the latest cholera epidemic – they get rotten diarrhoea, turn blue and then die.

1854 The last of London's great medieval fairs, Bartholomew Fair, is banned. People enjoy it too much!

1857 Indian rebels massacre bullying British rulers in India so British soldiers massacre Indians.

1870 An Education Act means school for everyone … and that means **YOU** … but it costs a penny a day.

1872 The empty ship, *Mary Celeste*, found adrift in the Atlantic – did the crew meet a gruesome end?

1879 The British army takes on the Zulus at Isandhlwana – the Zulus 'washed their spears' in British blood. Yeuch!

1883 Matthew Webb, who swam the English Channel in 1875, dies trying to swim rapids above Niagara Falls. Not a good idea.

1888 Jack the Ripper strikes in London – he is never caught.

1894 Blackpool Tower opens – a copy of the Eiffel Tower in Paris.

1897 Nine-year-old boy crushed by London taxi. First ever road death … of many.

1899 Percy Pilcher (honest, that's his name) flies in a hang glider – but not for long. Lands on head. Splatt. Dead.

Vile Victorian Queen

Victoria lost her father when she was eight months old. She lost her husband, Albert, when she was 42. The only thing she couldn't lose was her sense of humour … she never had one! Here are…

Ten things you should know about Victoria

1 Victoria's father was Edward Duke of Kent, the fourth son of George III. The playwright, Sheridan, suggested that Edward was bald because he hadn't enough brains inside his head to feed hair on the outside. What he actually said was, 'Grass does not grow upon deserts'.

2 She discovered she was heir to the throne when she was nearly eleven years old. She immediately promised, 'I will be good!' She meant, 'I will be a good little teacher's pet from now on.' Later, people twisted the meaning of these words and said she meant, 'I will be a good queen when I get my fat little bottom on the throne.'

3 Victoria could hardly wait. When the Lord Chamberlain brought her the news of William IV's death he ended by saying '…you are the Queen.' No sooner had he got the word 'Queen' out of his mouth than Victoria shot out a hand for him to kiss.

THAT WAS QUICK

ZIP!

4 The Queen did not grow to five feet tall – she made up for it by being about five feet wide in later life. Funnily enough this 'shortest' British monarch ruled 'longest' of any of them.

5 Victoria fell in love with her cousin Albert at first sight. She wrote … *Albert is really quite charming, and so excessively handsome, such beautiful blue eyes, an exquisite nose, and such a pretty mouth with delicate moustachios and slight but very slight whiskers; a beautiful figure, broad in the shoulders and a fine waist.* Soon after, Victoria proposed to Albert.

6 Albert died in 1861. A historian, Lytton Strachey, described Victoria's agony at Albert's death … *She shrieked – one long wild shriek that ran through the horror-stricken castle – and understood that she had lost him forever.* She became a changed woman. She refused for many years to appear in public. Then, when she did, she insisted on wearing her black widow's bonnet and not a crown.

7 Victoria spent much of her time in Scotland where she had a devoted manservant, John Brown. Rumours said that Brown had married Victoria (not true), that Victoria stopped him from marrying one of her maids (probably true) and that he was a 'Spiritualist' – he held seances in the room where Albert died and let Victoria talk to her dead husband (almost certainly not true!). He died in 1883.

8 The Queen's favourite Prime Minister was Benjamin Disraeli. In 1876 he had the Royal Titles Bill passed which made her Empress. (She was the first, last and only British Empress of India.) As Disraeli lay dying in 1881, someone suggested that the Queen should come and visit him. He replied, "She would only ask me to take a message to Albert."

'BETTER NOT, SHE WOULD ONLY ASK ME TO TAKE A MESSAGE TO ALBERT'

9 Victoria's least favourite Prime Minister was William Gladstone. She said he was 'half crazy and, really in many ways, a ridiculous old man.' The admiring public nicknamed him G.O.M. – Grand Old Man. Disraeli said it stood for God's Only Mistake!

10 Queen Vic survived seven attempts to assassinate her. The first three attempts took place in 1842. As the Queen rode in London's Mall with Albert, a man came out of the crowd and fired a pistol at her. He was just six or seven paces away. The gun misfired!

You would think Victoria would have learned her lesson. The very next day Victoria rode past the same spot ... and the same man fired again! The gun only had a blank in it, but John Francis, the gunman, was still sentenced to death. He was granted a reprieve before he was executed.

In July of that same year, a youth with a pathetic face fired at Queen Victoria as she was out riding in her carriage. Luckily for Queen Vic, the youth, John Bean, had put more paper and tobacco in the pistol than gunpowder.

Ten useless bits of information about Victoria…

1   Victoria had bishopophobia – a fear of bishops. When she was a little girl she was scared of their wigs. Her dislike of bishops lasted all her life.

2   As a child she could be a bad-tempered little madam. Her music teacher told her she 'must' practice the piano if she wanted to learn. She slammed the piano lid and snapped,

When she was playing with a friend she once said…

3 Victoria's coronation was quite an event, with the lords of the land queuing up to touch her crown as part of the ceremony. Some couldn't quite manage the last four steps up to the throne, as Harriet Martineau described…

Lord Rolle, a large and feeble old man, had to be held up by two lords. He had nearly reached the royal footstool when he slipped through the hands of the two lords and rolled over and over down the steps, lying at the bottom coiled up in his robes. He was instantly lifted up and he tried again and again amid shouts of admiration for his bravery. It turned me very sick.

One unkind witness suggested that he got the title of Lord 'Rolle' because of his coronation trick!

The ladies were as gruesome as the old lord. Harriet described them as...

Old hags, with their dyed or false hair drawn to the top of the head to allow them to put on their coronets. They had their necks and arms bare and glittering with diamonds; and those necks were so brown and wrinkled as to make one sick; or dusted over with white powder which was worse than what it disguised.

4 The coronation was curious in other ways. The Archbishop placed the coronation ring on the wrong finger and Victoria suffered 'great pain' in getting it off again. She went into a chapel at the side of the abbey where the Archbishop was supposed to give her the golden Orb. He couldn't. Victoria already had it!

The Queen's Treasurer scattered gold and silver medals among the lordly congregation ... but that caused a lot of 'turbulent scrimmaging' as they fought to pick them up! It was reported that...

The Aldermen of London sprawled over the floor in their furred gowns and grabbed one another by the sleeves in their rude scramble for the pieces.

tinkle
tinkle

158

5 Victoria's weight caused her adviser, Lord Melbourne, to nag her…

Lord Melbourne had no answer to that. Victoria didn't take up exercise. She got fat instead. The royal doctor said, 'She is more like a barrel than anything else.'

6 Queen Victoria's son-in-law, Prince Christian, was a truly vile Victorian. He lost an eye in a shooting accident. At dinner parties he would have a footman deliver his collection of glass eyes to the table. Christian would then tell the story of each eye. His favourite was the bloodshot one which he wore when he had a cold!

7 Victoria's most famous 'saying' is, 'We are not amused.' Her diaries are full of the phrase, 'I was very much amused,' but she never, ever said or wrote, 'We are not amused.' It's just a story! So there, now you know.

8 Old Victoria died in January 1901. She was buried with a picture of John Brown and a lock of his hair wrapped in tissue. The dead Queen's hair was cut off to be put into lockets for friends and family.

9 Victoria's vile son Edward became King Edward VII when she died. He was particularly fond of hunting. He once chased a deer from Harrow to Paddington where it was cornered at Paddington Station and killed as railway porters and guards watched. He shot down an elephant in Africa, hacked off its tail and jumped on its side to do a dance. But the elephant was only stunned, not dead. It rose to its feet and staggered off into the jungle … not wagging its tail! Edward wrote a letter home, complaining that the leeches in Africa 'climb up your legs and bight you.' He was even worse at spelling than he was at shooting elephants!

10 Victoria lived so long that Edward was an old man before he came to the throne. He complained…

I don't mind praying to the Eternal Father, but I must be the only man in the country plagued with an eternal mother.

Vile Victorian Childhood

Vile Victorian parents – or, Growing up is hard to do!

You may think your parents are pretty vile. They nag you to tidy your room, force you to eat your spinach and wear sensible clothes.

But at least you have some room, some food and some clothes! Many Victorian children weren't that lucky! When a new Victorian baby arrived, people would ask, 'Has it come to stay?' Growing up for many was like getting over an obstacle course of death.

MEET TINY TIM® THE NINETEENTH-CENTURY ACTION BABY – THE VICTORIAN TOT WITH A LOAD OF SURVIVING TO DO!

1 An 1860s report said...

In the last five years, in this district alone, at least 278 infants were murdered; more than 60 were found dead in the Thames or the canals or ponds of London and many more than a hundred were found dead, under railway arches, on doorsteps, in dustholes, cellars and the like.

And those were just the ones the police knew about. Many more babies suffocated at birth and the doctors didn't notice the cloth, dough or mud that had been used to smother them – 'Death by natural causes,' they said.

2 Let's face it – babies are smelly, noisy and expensive to keep. Some parents decided that the best way to deal with this was to send their child to a 'Baby Farm' – no that's not a nice place in the country like a sheep farm! A baby-farmer was a woman who would offer to look after your children for you. For five pounds you need never see your child again. Of course, the baby-farmer couldn't raise a child for life on five pounds, so the babies were neglected. If the baby died then that saved money. Baby-farmer, Margaret Walters, was brought to trial for her treatment of baby Cowan, who was described as...

scarcely a bit of flesh on the bones. It could only be recognised by the hair. It did not cry, being much too weak for that. It was scarcely human; I mean that it looked more like a monkey than a child. It was a shadow.

Baby Cowan died. Baby-farmer Walters was hanged.

3 You may object to sharing a bedroom with a grotty little brother. But in the 1860s, James Greenwood saw…

…grown persons sleeping with their parents, brothers and sisters, occupying the same bed of filthy rags or straw. I have note of a locality where 48 men, 73 women and 59 children are living in 34 rooms. In one house I found a single room with one man, two women and two children; and there was the dead body of a poor girl who had died a few days before. The body was stretched out on the bare floor without a shroud or coffin.

A French visitor, Hippolyte Taine, found a London family 'whose only bed was a heap of soot; they had been sleeping on it for some months.'

4 There wasn't enough food around to fatten a scavenging cat. Hippolyte said he saw…

A miserable black cat, skinny, limping, half stupefied. It was

watching an old woman fearfully out of one eye while sniffing and pawing through a pile of rubbish. No doubt it was right to be nervous – the old woman was watching it with a look as hungry as its own, and mumbling. It looked to me as if she were thinking there went two pounds of meat.

5   As soon as a child could crawl it could work. Making matchboxes was a boring, badly paid job, but at least children could do it from a very early age. If that was too boring then you could go on the street corners and sell the matches. You might not be able to afford shoes so you would freeze to death.

6   The young Doctor Barnardo from Dublin wanted to be a medical missionary in China. When he saw the state of the London children he decided he was more needed there. He opened homes for orphan children and educated them too. Many went to good jobs in England and abroad. Most of the girls went into service at the age of 16.

You've survived!

Getting a good job as a servant is proof that you've survived the Growing-up Game of life and death in London… But would you get that job? When you left Barnardo's you were placed in a division. Here are the four 'Divisions' you could be placed in at the age of 13… Which one would **YOU** end up in?

First Division:

All girls who, at 16, have a good record of conduct and character. They will receive an outfit worth five pounds which they can keep if they stay in their first job 12 months. If they have a good report after 12 months they will receive a special prize.

Second Division:

Girls who have frequently given way to ill temper, disobedience, insolence, laziness or other grave faults cannot be placed in the first division, but if they make a special effort in their final year to improve then they may be placed in the second division. They will receive an outfit worth three pounds and ten shillings and if they have a good report after 12 months will also receive a prize.

Third Division:

Girls who up to the time of their leaving continue to show bad conduct, ill temper, self-will, disobedience or insolence can only be placed in the third division with their mistress being informed of their faults. They will receive a third class outfit, value three pounds, the whole of which must be paid for out of their own wages. A girl in the third division will not be eligible for a prize till she has been in service two years and has earned a good report.

Fourth Division:

Girls who are found to be dishonest, regularly untruthful, violent and uncontrolled in temper, vicious, or unclean in their personal habits, will not be sent out to service, nor will they have an outfit but will be dismissed from Barnardo's in disgrace or sent to a school of discipline.

So? Where would **YOU** end up? And if you ended up in the first division would you **WANT** to be a maidservant in Victorian London? Here is a typical day.

A day in the life of a parlour maid – or, Is it worth going to bed?

Morning tasks

6.00 Get out of bed, wash dress, brush hair into a bun.

6.30 Go downstairs. Put the kettle on. Pull up blinds, open windows, clean fireplaces.

7.00 Make early tea and take it to master and mistress.

7.30 Sweep the dining room and dust. Lay the table for breakfast.

8.00 Serve breakfast.

8.30 Go upstairs, strip the beds, open the bedroom windows, have own breakfast.

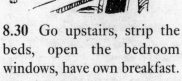

9.00 Clear breakfast table, wash up, put on clean apron, make the beds, clean the taps, wash the baths and bathroom floors, clean the toilets, dust every bedroom.

12.00 Change dress to serve lunch; lay the lunch table, serve the lunch, clear the table, wash up all the glass and silver, put everything away in its place.

1.00 Clean the pantry sink and floor, eat own lunch.

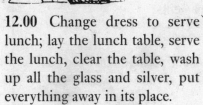

ᘒDAILY GRIND REMINDERᘓ
2·00 pm – 6·00 pm

Monday: Help with laundry, wash brushes and combs, clear out pantry
Make sure to get the grease off the master's combs

Tuesday: Clear out dining room, clean windows, clean fireplaces
~~after fireplace~~ WASH HANDS before cleaning windows

Wednesday: Clear out a bedroom and a dressing room
Mistress's bedroom, keep the cat out

Thursday: Clean all the silver cutlery, plates and ornaments
Polish the Master's domino trophies v. carefully

Friday: Clean toilets, passage, stairs and hall
don't forget the fiddly bits

Saturday: Clean out servants' bedrooms
do Cook's first OR ELSE!!!
Cook

Sunday: Afternoon off
(sleep)

Evening tasks

6.00 Lay the table for dinner.

7.00 Serve dinner and wait at table.

8.30 Clear dinner table, wash up.

10.00 Eat own supper, wash up.

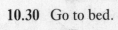

10.30 Go to bed.

Next day ... start all over again. Of course, you would be paid. Paid nearly six pounds – six pounds a **YEAR** that is! And that's what you'd get for being a **GOOD** girl!

Five rules for servants

1 No followers - that is to say, no boyfriends for the maidservants. The mistress of the house didn't want strange men hanging around and she didn't want anyone getting married so she lost their services just as she had got them fully trained.

2 No dishonesty - a common trick was for the mistress to hide a coin under a carpet. If the servant didn't find the coin then she hadn't done the sweeping properly - she'd be sacked; if she **did** find the coin and kept it then, of course, she'd be sacked for dishonesty!

DON'T OVER-DO IT DEAR !

3 Wear a uniform - men had to wear dark suits or evening dress; women had to buy (or make) a cotton dress for morning wear and a black wool dress with a white cap and apron for the afternoons. (As a special treat she might be given some cloth as a Christmas present to make a new dress!)

4 Stay invisible - servants were to keep out of the way as much as possible; if a lady or gentleman of the house appeared, they had to stand aside to let them pass.

5 Stay fit - a sick servant cost money to keep fed and housed. The ill or the very old would usually be dismissed to make room for a fitter or younger person.

So, life as a servant could be hard and the hours long. But at least the work wasn't usually **dangerous**. Life in the coal mines, on the other hand, could be positively deadly – even for children…

The Monster of the mine
I

'Deep below the ground there's a great dark monster,' Granny Milburn mumbled through her toothless mouth.

'What does it look like?' Geordie asked.

'No one knows. They never see it, only hear its rattling roar and then its iron claws strike sparks from off the railway lines!' the old woman said and scrubbed her grandson's skinny back as he shivered in the old tin bath.

'And what does this dark monster do?'

'It eats up little boys that fall asleep below the ground,' she warned.

'But just the ones that fall asleep?'

'Yes. Just the ones that fall asleep!'

'But is this story true, Gran?' little Geordie breathed and his big grey eyes glinted fearful in the firelight.

The woman helped her grandson from the bath and rubbed him with a dry cloth. 'You had a brother, Tommy, once. He was just your age – just eight years old. One day he went off down the mine. He never came back home.'

'What happened, Gran? The monster? Did it get him?' young Geordie cried, and shuddered in his nightshirt.

'What's all this talk of monsters?' Geordie's mam asked as she came into the room. Her arms were full of cold, wet washing which she spread on some wooden rails above the fire to dry.

'Our Granny says there's monsters down the mine,' the boy said.

'Don't listen to your Gran!' his mam said wearily. 'You're eight years old – too old for fairy tales … we need the money that you'll get down Burnhope pit. Ten pence every week while your poor dad's laid off with coal dust in his chest.'

'I know, mam … and I want to work. It's just I'm scared the monster's going to get me!'

'Now get to bed!' his mother snapped and pushed him to the door. 'And don't you wake your father up or else he'll take his belt to you!'

'I won't, mam! Night Gran!'

'Good night, boy!' Granny Milburn sighed, then muttered, 'God preserve you down that mine.'

Geordie took a candle and stepped around his dad who snored upon some straw-sacks on the floor. The boy slipped between his three young sisters and his baby brother. His mother wrapped a blanket round his body and whispered, 'I'll wake you up at three o'clock tomorrow morning. Sleep well.'

As she left, the boy said, 'Mam!'

'Yes, Geordie?'

'Can I take some candles down the mine?' he begged.

The woman shook her head. 'They cost more than a penny every day! You'll spend most of your wages just on light!'

'Please mam!' Geordie asked. 'Just until I get used to the work.'

'All right! But just for one week and then no more!' she warned and blew her candle out.

II

Mister Wilson's boots clacked crisply on the cobbles while Geordie stumbled on and tried to stay in step.

'Am I to be a trapper?' Geordie panted.

'You are,' the man said briskly.

'What do trappers have to do?' the boy asked. 'Do they have to trap things?'

He stepped into the cage, crammed amongst the men, and gasped as it dropped suddenly into the blackness. The air rushed upwards, smelling hot and damp and choking Geordie. After half a minute the cage jolted to a stop. Geordie's knees were weaker than his cold tea.

He staggered out into the cave. The candles of the men sparkled in a line like a necklace of light as they set off along the tunnel.

'This is the horse-way,' Mister Wilson said.

Geordie nodded. Horses clattered past with wagons full of coal to load into the cage. 'So where do I work?' Geordie dared to ask.

'Another mile,' the tall man answered.

A mile! Geordie's little legs could never walk a mile! He trudged on after Mister Wilson. Men began to disappear down some passages that opened from the side walls of the horse-way. At last they were alone. The grey-faced overman pointed down a passage. 'Turn off down this barrow-way!'

The barrow-way was narrow and the darkest place that Geordie had ever been. Mister Wilson's candle glinted on the dark, damp walls and on the iron railway lines that

ran along the floor.

At last the light shone on a wooden door. Mr Wilson turned and faced the boy. The candle shone up on his thin grey face, casting shadows in his tired red eyes. He pointed to the door.

'That's your trap!' the tall man said. 'You open it by pulling on this string. Here, try.'

Geordie pulled the string and watched the wood door open. 'It's there to keep the air out of the barrow-way. See?' the overman said.

'Yes,' young Geordie said, although he didn't really.

'The door has to stay closed,' the man went on. 'But of course it has to open when the trucks or barrows come along. That's your job – to open the door. And if a miner comes along and you aren't there and ready then he'll give you such a beating!' Mister Wilson warned.

'Is that what happened to our Tommy?' Geordie asked.

The man leaned forward and he peered hard in Geordie's face. 'No, lad. Tommy didn't wander off from duty. Tommy did a much worse thing!'

The young boy wondered what could be much worse. 'What was that?' he asked.

Mister Wilson spoke slowly and quite cruelly. 'What young Tommy Milburn did was simply fall asleep.'

'Fall asleep!' young Geordie squeaked. His mouth went dry. Fall asleep! The monster must have got him.

'He fell asleep. He fell asleep and fell across the line. The next time a truck came by, it … urrgh!' the tall man shuddered. He put his hand on Geordie's shoulder and led him to a little hole hacked in the side of the barrow-way wall. A hole no bigger than the kitchen fireplace far above in Geordie's home. 'You sit in here … now, take the string … the first truck should be down in half an hour.'

And then he left and took his candle with him. 'Mister Wilson!' Geordie called. His words just echoed off the empty walls. He had a pocket full of candles but nothing to light one with.

He sat there in the dark and he'd never felt so lonely in all his eight years.

His eyes grew used to the dark but he couldn't get used to the quietness. The odd drips of water made him jump. A steady thumping noise turned out to be his own heart.

Sometimes the voices of men drifted to his door. But all the time he waited for the rattle and the roar of the great dark monster.

Geordie tried to sing a song he'd learned in Sunday school, but his dry mouth croaked a miserable sound and he gave up. He closed his tired eyes and thought about the Sunday school. The summer trips down to the river. The warm sun and the picnic food. He could smell the sweet grass and feel the cool water.

And the thoughts drifted into dreams as Geordie fell asleep! But when he'd fallen deep asleep the nightmare monster came to haunt him. He heard the rattle and the roar and then he thought he saw his Granny saying, 'Only boys who fall asleep! Only boys who fall asleep!'

He forced his tired eyes open. The rattle and the roar was real enough! His head was lying on the track and that whole track was shaking. Sparks were flying off the track and Geordie jerked his head back just in time. He hauled the string, the trap flew open and the heavy truck rushed by! 'Well done, young 'un!' a miner cried before he vanished in the black.

III

'They don't have monsters down the mine,' he told his granny as she tucked him in that night. 'They just have trucks that rush along.'

Granny Milburn nodded wisely. 'Sparking on the iron rails and rattling and a-roaring! That's what Tommy said. Just like monsters.'

'But still,' he yawned, 'that story saved my life! The nightmare woke me up in time! I'll never fall asleep again.'

Granny grinned and showed her pale pink gums. 'Yes you will,' she said. 'You'll fall asleep before the clock strikes ten!'

'I mean,' the boy began to murmur. 'I mean … at work… '

The woman tucked his blanket in and ran her old hand through his new-washed hair. 'Sleep well,' she said.

Did you know…?
In 1842 the law was changed. Children under ten years of age, and women, were no longer allowed to work in the mines.

Vile Victorian names

Victorian parents could be cruel to their children in many ways. For example, they could torture them for life by giving them a terrible name. Which of the following names were given to Victorian children?

Vile Victorian child labour … or, Wouldn't you rather stay at home?

Home life was not easy. With parents and elder brothers and sisters at work for most of the day, you could find yourself left at home to care for toddlers and babies. George Simms in 1881 describes a typical life of one such carer.

There she sat, in the bare squalid room, perched on a sack, erect, motionless, expressionless, on duty … left to guard a baby that lay asleep on the bare boards behind her, its head on its arm, the ragged remains of what had been a shawl flung over its legs.

Question: How old was this girl?

Answer: Four years old.

If you were not lucky enough to find work as a servant, or in the mines or factories, you could find other ways to earn your keep. Here are some examples. Which do you prefer?

Nail making

On average a child would earn three to four shillings a week if his nails were good quality. If not, he could expect a severe beating, or something much worse…

Somebody in the warehouse took him and put his head down on an iron counter and hammered a nail through his ear, and the boy has made good nails ever since.

Children's Employment Commission (1842)

Chimney sweeping

This was a popular job for young boys and girls, who were chosen for their size and agility.

Life was cruel and conditions were vile. Working in hot, dark and cramped conditions was very hard and tiring. Children often scraped their elbows and knees as they climbed up inside the chimneys. One sweep said…

No one knows the cruelty they undergo in learning. The flesh must be hardened. This is done by rubbing it, chiefly on the elbows and the knees, with the strongest brine (salt water) close by a hot fire. You must stand over them with a cane…

But beware! Any of you who think this job was easy, think again! If a worker was found sleeping on the job, or if by his own misfortune he became stuck in the chimney, his master would light a fire beneath him!

Ribbon making

You may think that making ribbons for the hair and the dresses of ladies was a pleasant, gentle occupation? Think again!

Three hundred boys were employed in turning hand looms. The endless whirl had such a bad effect on the head and the stomach that the little turners often suffered in the brain and the spinal cord and some died of it. In one mill near Cork six deaths and 60 mutilations have occurred in four years.

Victorian observer

183

Vile Victorian schools

So you have to go to school? Blame the Vile Victorians! In 1870 the Education Bill was passed. The aim was ... *to bring education within the reach of every English home, aye, and within the reach of those children who have no homes.*

Children of the 1990s still suffer the horror of homework, the terror of teachers and the dread of school dinners. But, if you think school is bad in the 20th century, you should have gone to school in the 19th!

Here are four school sins. What punishment would you give for each one?

Make the punishment fit the crime

1 Throwing ink pellets in class, punished by...
a) A severe talking-to by the teacher
b) Kneeling on the floor with your hands behind your head
c) A treble helping of lumpy mashed potato at school dinner

2 Missing Sunday church, punished by…

a) A severe talking-to by the priest and detention while you listen to the sermon you missed

b) A beating with a strap

c) Doing extra work for the church - polishing the candlesticks, digging a few graves, copying out the Bible, etc

3 Being late for school, punished by…

a) Having your name written in the Punishment Book so you may not get a job when you leave school

b) Being hit over the hand with a cane

c) Both

4 Ink blots and fingermarks on work, punished by…

a) Being caned (so your hands are sore and you probably make even more mess)

b) Having to do the work again

c) Death

Answers:

1 b) Kneeling

One punishment was to kneel on the hard, rough floorboards, with your back upright and your hands placed on the back of your neck for a long period of about twenty minutes. Should you lop over, aching all over, the teacher would slap you across the head with his hand and shout sternly, 'Get upright, will you?'

Victorian boy

2 b) The strap

Every Monday morning the priest came to each class and asked us who had missed church the day before. I always had to miss Sunday because Sunday was washing day and we only had one lot of clothes. So, week by week we admitted our absence and were given the strap for it. We should have been able to explain but we were ashamed to give the real reason. Once, just once, I answered back.

'Don't you know,' the priest said, 'that God loves you and wants to see you in His house on Sundays?'

'But if he loves us, why does he want us to get the strap on Monday?' I asked.

I don't remember what the priest said, but I do know I got a double load of stripes when he'd gone.

Victorian girl

3 c) The punishment book

With no exams at the end of your school life, the chance of a good job after school depended on your final report - your reference. One boy was kept back by his father and so he was late for school...

186

The only boy in the school to be late. I was humiliated in front of three hundred boys by the headmaster and afterwards got six mighty slashes on the fingers with a thin cane. My God, it hurt, believe me. And something else which hurt even more. My name was inserted in the disgrace and punishment book and put on record for future reference.

Victorian boy

4 a)   The cane

Some teachers chose specially thin canes because they hurt more. Many a time the cane would be broken over the hand (or bottom) of the pupil. Caning still went on in English schools more than eighty years after Victoria died. (Ask your parents!)

The terrible teachers' top ten facts

1 One of the most famous teachers in the 19th century was William Shaw. But he was famous for all the wrong reasons. Shaw was the headmaster of Bowes Academy in North Yorkshire. The writer Charles Dickens heard about Shaw when the headmaster's bad treatment landed him in court. Shaw was so cruel that two of his pupils lost their sight.

Dickens visited the school in 1837 and observed the man. He then created the villainous headmaster, Wackford Squeers, in his book *Nicholas Nickleby*. Everybody knew that Wackford Squeers was really William Shaw.

The publication of the book ruined Shaw's business. He died in 1850. Serves him right? End of story? Not quite. Some of the local people of Bowes thought that Dickens had been unfair to Shaw. They dedicated a window to Shaw in the local church after his death.

2 Some vile Victorian teachers didn't believe in talking to pupils to find out why they did something wrong. They simply punished them. Teachers had a motto…

For bad boys a yard of strap is worth a mile of talk.

I THINK IT'S THE OTHER WAY ROUND

3 Teachers could train by working in the classroom with an older teacher. Trainee teachers started at the age of 14.

4 Trainees could go to college. Some college rules were worse than school rules! At one men's college, the trainee teachers could...

not leave the college except at certain times
not go to the bedrooms during the day
not stay up after 10:00 p.m.
not have a light on in their bedroom
not go to any public house
not smoke
not make friends with the local people

FUN, FUN, FUN

And they had to take some form of active exercise every afternoon!

5 The Victorians believed that boys should be treated differently from girls ... and that men were more important than women. This showed in the schools.

In 1870, women teachers were paid 58 pounds a year... but men were paid 94!

Boys' lessons included carpentry, farmwork, gardening, shoe making, drawing, handicrafts.

Girls' lessons included housewifery (sweeping, dusting, making beds and bathing a baby), needlework and cookery.

6 Cookery lessons were difficult in poorer schools where pupils couldn't afford the ingredients. An inspector once made a report on a class of girls who had a lesson on roasting meat. One single chop was prepared and cooked by 18 girls!

7 Lessons were often just learning things by heart, then repeating them. A typical (horrible) history lesson went like this:

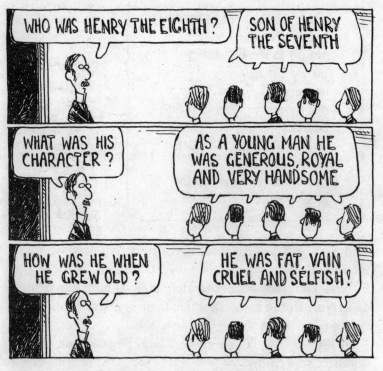

8 Reading books were even worse! Children learned to read from books which had wonderful lines like…

Do not nod on a sod.

Can a ram sit on a sod?

Let Sam sip the sap of the red jam.

9 There were often as many as 70 or 80 pupils in one class. The teachers would have to shout or even scream to be heard above the noise of the children. One doctor had so many teachers complaining of sore throats he called it, 'Board School Laryngitis'!

10 Punishments were given in factories to get the most work possible from a child. One man, Joseph Lancaster, invented a similar system of punishments which was used in some schools. (They are quite vile, so please don't try them out on your teacher!)

'The log' A piece of wood weighing four to six pounds was tied across the shoulders of the offending child so that, when he moved, the log acted as a dead weight. It was a punishment for talking, which often didn't work, as the child would be in floods of noisy tears.

'Pillory and stocks' Unlike earlier times, children who suffered this 'pleasure' were not pelted by rotten tomatoes. They were put in the stocks, left and forgotten about.

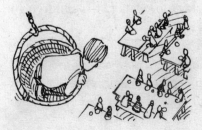

'The cage' This was a basket suspended from the ceiling, into which the more serious offenders were put.

Vile Victorian schools – six of the best

Did you know…?

1 Many parents couldn't afford to send their children to the new Board Schools set up in the 1870s. It wasn't just the penny a week they had to pay - it was the fact that children weren't free to help their mothers with the housework, or earn the family extra money by working.

2 Some schools had special offers like, 'Three for the price of two'. If there were three children in a family at school, then the parents paid for the first two and the third could go free.

3 Some parents blamed teachers for making the children go to school. One teacher wrote…

I well remember how, early in my career as a teacher, I had to avoid various missiles thrown at me by angry parents who would rather have the children running errands or washing up things in the home than wasting their time in school with such things as learning.

4 If a parent didn't want to send their child to school, they would say that the child was ill. A School Board Inspector would have to go to check if the 'illness' went on too long. One inspector was told that a child was dead – when he visited the house he found the 'dead' child was so well she was skipping in the middle of the living-room floor!

5 School Board Inspectors were so unpopular in some areas that they had to go around in pairs – to protect each other from angry parents!

6 School Dinners – 1885 style

~ MENU ~

PENNY DINNER
Boiled Pork, meat pudding, vegetables

FARTHING DINNER
Soup, bread and jam

FREE DINNER
Cup of cocoa or soup made from boiling meat bones

Vile Victorian fun and games

Some games you could try

Geordie bowling

Each competitor has a ball of clay the size of a tennis ball – or a rag ball, or a bean bag if you prefer.

1 Taking turns, throw your ball as far as you can.
2 Collect it and throw it again … and again … and again until you reach the end of the course. (Geordies threw them for a mile – you could try the length of your school playing field.)
3 The one who reaches the end with the fewest throws is the winner.

Up the buttons

1 Everyone needs a collection of buttons (or counters) to play with. Make sure you can each identify which are your own.
2 Mark a large chalk square on the pavement near the wall of a house.
3 Mark the word 'OXO' in the centre.
4 Decide how many buttons each person is going to play (say 10).
5 Each player (say 6) places their buttons along the kerb in line with the square.
6 Take turns to flick each button forward (with thumb and finger)
7 After all the buttons have been flicked into the square, the player whose button is nearest the 'X' of the OXO is the winner.
8 The winner gathers up all the buttons.

Vile Victorian games you must never ever try!

1 Only the very rich had proper toilets with water to wash the contents into the sewers. The poor had to make do with a small building at the bottom of the yard. There was a wooden bench with a hole in it. Underneath were ashes from the fire. Once a week the ashes would be collected by Night Soil Men and taken away on a cart to be dumped.

But ... some vile Victorian children took sticks and dipped them in the waste. They then carried the dirty sticks to the posher streets and wiped them on the door-knockers of the houses!

ARE WE PLAYING POOH STICKS?

2 A popular trick was to tie two door-knockers together across the street, rap on the doors, then hide and watch as the two house owners struggled against each other to open the doors!

Some sports you would find very vile

Ratting

Bets are placed on how many rats a dog can kill in a given amount of time. The fight takes place in a large rat pit.

A 19th-century visitor describes a ratting event…

The floor was swept and a big, flat basket produced, like those in which chickens are brought to market. Under the top can be seen a small mound of closely packed rats. This match seemed to be between the rat-pit owner and his son. The bet was a bottle of lemonade. It was strange to watch the daring manner in which the lad pushed his hand into the rat cage and fumbled about and stirred up with his fingers the living mass, picking up only the big ones, as he'd been told.

When 50 animals had been flung into the pit they gathered themselves into a mound which reached one third up the sides. They were all sewer and waterditch rats and the smell that rose from them was like that from a hot drain.

The moment the terrier was loose he buried his nose in the mound till he brought one out in his mouth. In a short time a dozen rats were lying bleeding on the floor and the white paint of the pit became grained with blood.

In a little time the terrier had a rat hanging on to his nose which, despite his tossing, still held on. He dashed up against the sides of the pit, leaving a patch of blood as if a strawberry had been smashed there.

'Time!' called the owner. The dog was caught and held, panting, his neck stretched out like a serpent's, staring at the rats that still kept crawling about.

The lad with the rats asked, 'Would any gentleman like any rats?'

Boxing

No gloves. No real rules, except you don't kick an opponent when they're on the ground. The winner is the one left standing at the end. Women's boxing was common. Large crowds would gather when a challenge was issued…

> 'I Elizabeth Wilkinson of Clerkenwell, having had angry words with Hannah Highfield, do invite her to meet me on the stage and box for three guineas. Each woman is to hold a half-crown coin in each hand The first woman that drops her money loses the battle'.
>
> E Wilkinson

The reply came…

> 'I Hannah Highfield of Newgate Market, hearing the challenge of Elizabeth Wilkinson, will not fail, God willing, to give her more blows than words.'
>
> H Highfield

Vile Victorian sportsmen

The Eighth Earl of Bridgewater was fond of shooting. But when his eyesight began to fade, he had the wings of pigeons clipped to slow them down. That way they were easier to hit! But at least the Earl loved his dogs…

He had soft leather boots made for them to protect their paws.

He took half a dozen of them for rides in his carriage each day.

He dined with twelve of them every night in the great hall of his house.

Each dog had a clean white napkin round its neck. Servants stood behind them, dishing out food onto the family's silver plates while the Earl chatted to the dogs politely.

And if you think he was odd, what about the Second Baron Rothschild? He had a carriage drawn by four zebras. Snakes twined themselves around the bannisters of the stairway in his house.

A tame bear had a habit of slapping lady guests on the bottom. Twelve dinner guests found they had 12 beautifully dressed partners sitting next to them–they were monkeys!

A question of Victorian sport

1 Matthew Webb was the first man to achieve a great feat in 1875. The Mayor of Dover welcomed him and announced…

I make so bold as to say that I don't believe, in the future history of the world, any such feat will be performed by anybody else.

He was wrong! What did Matthew Webb do?

2 Blackburn Rovers had to play a soccer match against Burnley in 1891. It had been snowing for three hours before the game. The Blackburn team weren't too keen to turn out. By half time they were three goals down. For the second half only seven players bothered to leave the warmth of the dressing room.

Ten minutes later, Lofthouse, one of the Blackburn players, smacked the face of the Burnley captain. The Burnley captain hit him back. They were both sent off. The Blackburn players followed them – except the goalkeeper, Clegg. Burnley played on and scored. The Blackburn goalkeeper claimed the goal was offside. He was right. The referee abandoned the game.

But why had the Blackburn players walked off?

3 In 1885, in Scotland, the team Bon Accord stayed on the pitch even though they were losing ten-nil at half time. After the break they got tired and gave away even more goals. The final score is the greatest ever recorded in a professional soccer match.

What was that score?

4 In 1894, a cricket record was broken in Australia - the highest number of runs scored from a single ball. The ball was hit in the air and landed in the forked branch of a tree. The batsmen started to run. Two fielders climbed the tree. A branch snapped and they fell out. The batsmen ran on. The fielding team decided to chop the tree down - they wasted a lot of time looking for an axe. The batsmen ran on. The fielding team found some guns and shot the branches off the tree. By the time the ball fell to earth, the batting team had declared and had gone for tea.

But how many runs had they scored?

5 The first cyclist to take a long-distance ride ended in Glasgow, where he knocked down a little boy in the street. He was taken to court and the magistrate fined him five shillings. But who paid the fine?

6 The Duke of Beaufort liked to play 'real' (or indoor) tennis at his stately home. He played in the picture gallery of the house but gave up. The ball was wrecking the precious oil paintings on the walls. Instead he played a similar game but replaced the ball with something else. The game had been played in India, where it was known as Poona. But Victorian people who learned to play it named the game after the Duke of Beaufort's house. We still play The Duke's game today.

But what do we call it?

Vile Victorian poems, plays and songs

If the Victorians had a favourite subject, then it was Death. There was nothing they liked better than a sad story of suffering, heartbreak, tragedy and cruelty. The trouble was it was not just the subjects that were painful. The writing was pretty bad too! The Victorian ballad writers were probably the world's worst poets.

Vile Victorian love songs

No radio or television, no records or tapes. How did the Victorians entertain themselves at home? The middle classes would buy a piano, learn to play it and then sing some songs. Love songs were as popular then as they are today, but can you imagine standing by the family piano and singing this?

That is Love
See the father standing at his cottage door,
Watching the baby in the gutter rolling o'er,
Laughing at his merry pranks, but hark! A roar!
Help! Oh, help him! Gracious Heav'n above!
Dashing down the road there comes a maddened horse!
Out the father rushes with resistless force.
Saves the child ... but he lies there, a mangled corpse.
That is love, that is love!

If that's not cheerful enough for you, then you may prefer a children's song. The moral of the song is that death's not really that bad if you've behaved yourself in this life...

Shall I be an Angel, Daddy?

One day a father to his little son
Told a sad story, a heart-breaking one,
He took from an album a photo, and said,
'This is your mother, but she's been long dead;
You she has left me to cherish and love,
She is an angel, my child, up above.'
The boy in an instant drew close to his side,
And these are the words that he softly replied…

Chorus:
Shall I be an angel, daddy?
An angel in the sky?
Will I wear the golden wings,
And rest in peace on high?
Shall I live forever and ever
With the angels fair?
If I go to heaven, oh! tell me, Daddy,
Will I see Mother there?

Are the tears running down your legs? Or do you just feel sick? Perhaps you'd be better getting out of the house and going to the theatre.

205

Vile victorian plays

The theatres were very popular. So popular that they built huge ones to fit all the people in. If your seat was at the back, then you were a long way from the actors, of course. Never mind. The actors shouted all their lines and made huge gestures with their hands. In fact they over-acted like mad so that everyone got the point.

The plays were written to match this style. Simple plots and characters. Baddies were bad and goodies were good. You booed and hissed the villain and cheered for the hero. This style of theatre was known as 'Melodrama'. Songs were mixed with the action.

And the message's were simple too. In *Ten Nights in a Bar-Room*, written by William W. Pratt in 1858, the message was simply, 'Don't drink alcohol.' Here is the most touching scene – have a tissue handy to wipe away your tears...

SCENE: Interior of the *Sickle and Sheaf* Public House. Joe Morgan is drinking with his friends, including Simon Slade, the landlord. Little Mary Morgan is outside the door.

Mary: (Crying) Father! Father! Where is my father? (Enter Mary - she runs to Morgan)
Oh! I've found you, at last! Now won't you come home with me?

Morgan: Blessings on thee, my little one! Darkly shadowed is the sky that hangs gloomily over thy young head.

Mary: Come, father, mother has been waiting a long time, and I left her crying so sadly. Now do come home and make us all so happy.

Mary: (singing)

Father, dear father, come home with me now!
The clock in the steeple strikes one.
You promised, dear father, that you would come home
As soon as your day's work was done;
Our fire has gone out - our house is all dark-
And mother's been watching since tea,
With poor brother Benny so sick in her arms,
And no one to help her but me.

Chorus:

Come home, come home, come home,
Please father, dear father, come home.
Hear the sweet voice of the child,
Which the night winds repeat as they roam!
Oh! Who could resist this most plaintive of prayers?
Please, father, dear father, come home.

Father, dear father, come home with me now!
The clock in the steeple strikes two;
The night has grown colder and Benny is worse–
But he has been calling for you.
Indeed he is worse – Ma says he will die,
Perhaps before morning shall dawn;
And this is the message she sent me to bring:
'Come quickly or he will be gone.'
Chorus:
Come home...

Father, dear father, come home with me now!
The clock in the steeple strikes three;
The house is so lonely – the hours are so long
For poor weeping mother and me.
Yes, we are alone – poor Benny is dead,
And gone with the angels of light;
And these were the very last words that he said–
'I want to kiss Papa goodnight!'
Chorus:
Come home...

Morgan: (Suddenly realising the evil of his drinking habit)

Yes, my child, I'll go. (Kisses her) You have robbed me of my last penny, Simon Slade, but this treasure still remains. Farewell, friend Slade. (To Mary) Come, dear one, come. I'll go home. Come, come! I'll go, yes, I'll go.

(Exit Morgan and Mary)

Happy ending – except for poor Benny, of course? No chance. Later in the drama, a glass is thrown at Morgan. It misses him – and hits little Mary on the head instead. She dies while singing a hymn to her grief-stricken parents. As Morgan collapses on the couch and Mrs Morgan sobs over the body, the curtain falls.

NOW the Victorian audience could go home happy! They could also go to the pub. In London, one house in every 77 was reckoned to be a public house. In part of Newcastle, there was one pub for every 22 families.

Mr Morgan could well have drunk a lot of beer. Dishonest landlords like Slade would add salt to the beer, so the more you drank the thirstier you got! (Today they have crisps and peanuts instead!)

Vile Victorian books

But it wasn't just the popular writers who loved sentimental mush. The 'serious' writers were at it too. The ones your teachers call 'Classical' - people like Charles Dickens...

The Old Curiosity Shop

(The boy Kit has come to visit his friend Little Nell. She's as dead as a rocking-horse's hoof, but her aged father doesn't want to believe it.)

'Where is she?' demanded Kit. 'Oh tell me but that - but that, dear master!'

'She is asleep – yonder – in there.'*

'Thank God!'

'Ay! Thank God!' returned the old man. 'I have prayed to him many, and many, and many a livelong night, when she has been asleep. She is sleeping soundly,' he said; 'but no wonder. Angel hands have strewn the ground deep with snow so that the lightest footsteps may be lighter yet; and even the birds are dead so that they may not wake her.** She used to feed them. The timid things would fly from us. They never flew from her.'

Kit had no power to speak. His eyes were filled with tears.***

For she was dead.**** There upon the little bed she lay at rest.

She was dead. No sleep so beautiful and calm, so free from trace of pain, so fair to look upon.

She was dead. Dear, gentle, patient, noble Nell was dead.

Where were the traces of her early cares, her sufferings, her fatigues? All gone.

And still her former self lay there. Yes. The old fireside had smiled upon that same sweet face. At the still bedside of the dying boy there had been the same mild, lovely look. So shall we see the angels in their majesty after death.

The old man looked in agony to those who stood around as if imploring them to help her. She was dead, and past all help or need of it.

She had been dead two days.

* Being dead as a duck's toe nail she will get one heck of a shock when she tries to wake up.
** But not as dead as Little Nell!
*** He's guessed!
**** I told you so!

Vile Victorian poetry

And the most respected of Victorian poets, Alfred, Lord Tennyson, the Poet Laureate. His most popular poem was *In Memoriam*, written in memory of his dead friend, Arthur. Queen Victoria loved it! It drones on for hundreds and hundreds of verses about death. Verses like…

> *I sing to him that rests below,*
> *And, since the grasses round me wave,*
> *I take the grasses of the grave,*
> *And make them pipes whereon to blow.*

Can you imagine that … taking grass off a grave to make a pipe to play?

At least some Victorian poets could laugh at the serious ones with hilarious poems that made fun of the tragic ones…

Mr Jones by Harry Graham (1899)

> *'There's been an accident!' they said,*
> *'Your servant's cut in half; he's dead!'*
> *'Indeed!' said Mr Jones, 'and please*
> *Send me the half that's got my keys.'*

Vile Victorian Life

The industrial revolution

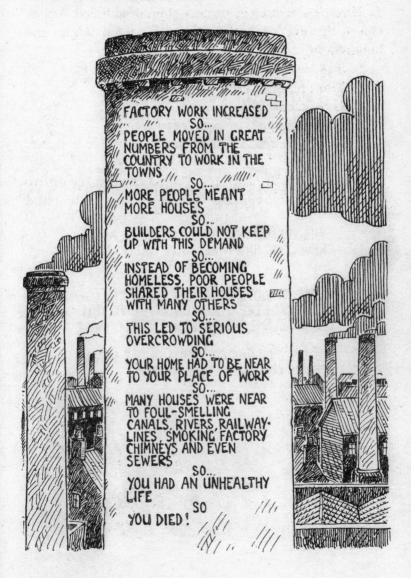

FACTORY WORK INCREASED
SO...
PEOPLE MOVED IN GREAT NUMBERS FROM THE COUNTRY TO WORK IN THE TOWNS
SO...
MORE PEOPLE MEANT MORE HOUSES
SO...
BUILDERS COULD NOT KEEP UP WITH THIS DEMAND
SO...
INSTEAD OF BECOMING HOMELESS, POOR PEOPLE SHARED THEIR HOUSES WITH MANY OTHERS
SO...
THIS LED TO SERIOUS OVERCROWDING
SO...
YOUR HOME HAD TO BE NEAR TO YOUR PLACE OF WORK
SO...
MANY HOUSES WERE NEAR TO FOUL-SMELLING CANALS, RIVERS, RAILWAY-LINES, SMOKING FACTORY CHIMNEYS AND EVEN SEWERS
SO...
YOU HAD AN UNHEALTHY LIFE
SO
YOU DIED!

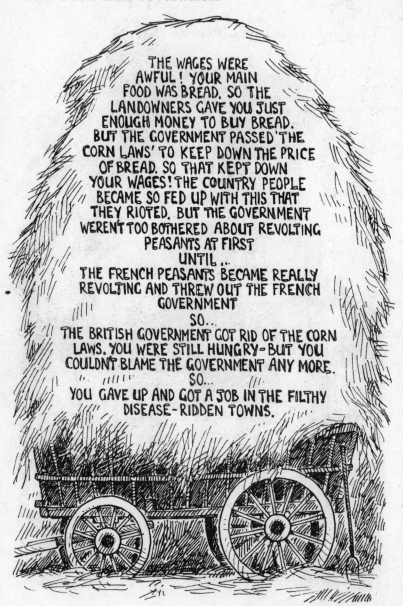

THE WAGES WERE AWFUL! YOUR MAIN FOOD WAS BREAD. SO THE LANDOWNERS GAVE YOU JUST ENOUGH MONEY TO BUY BREAD. BUT THE GOVERNMENT PASSED 'THE CORN LAWS' TO KEEP DOWN THE PRICE OF BREAD. SO THAT KEPT DOWN YOUR WAGES! THE COUNTRY PEOPLE BECAME SO FED UP WITH THIS THAT THEY RIOTED. BUT THE GOVERNMENT WEREN'T TOO BOTHERED ABOUT REVOLTING PEASANTS AT FIRST

UNTIL...

THE FRENCH PEASANTS BECAME REALLY REVOLTING AND THREW OUT THE FRENCH GOVERNMENT

SO...

THE BRITISH GOVERNMENT GOT RID OF THE CORN LAWS. YOU WERE STILL HUNGRY - BUT YOU COULDN'T BLAME THE GOVERNMENT ANY MORE.

SO...

YOU GAVE UP AND GOT A JOB IN THE FILTHY DISEASE-RIDDEN TOWNS.

1. Carter   2. Blacksmith   3. Pedlar
4. Mower   5. Milkmaid
6. Mole-catcher   7. Shepherd.

Ten foul facts on vile Victorian towns

1 All the sewage of Cambridge used to flow into the river, which made it a pretty disgusting place to walk beside. In 1843, Queen Victoria was walking beside the river when she asked one of the university teachers an embarrassing question.

'WHAT ARE THOSE PIECES OF PAPER FLOATING DOWN THE RIVER ?'

'THOSE, MADAM, ARE NOTICES SAYING THAT BATHING IS FORBIDDEN'

2 In 1853 a cholera epidemic in London killed 11,500. London's drains carried sewage and germs straight into the river Thames. The river water was then used for washing clothes and even cooking! The Thames was such a stinking sewer in the hot summer of 1858 that the blinds of the Houses of Parliament had to be soaked in chloride of lime so that the MPs could meet without choking on the smell.

3 Until the mid 1860s, London relied on water pumped from the river Thames as its main source. But up to 200 sewers emptied into it! Raw sewage could be seen coming out of standpipes in the streets of London, and out of kitchen taps in the houses of the rich, the water flowed a 'healthy' brown colour! In London, an Inspector in 1847 discovered that sewage was a problem which would not go away on its own. He reported…

The filth was lying scattered around the rooms, vaults, cellars and yards, so thick and so deep, that it was hardly possible to move through it.

4 Some men were given the job of clearing rubbish from the river Thames … and for recovering dead bodies. There was a reward for finding a missing person, but the Thames body-finders had an extra reward - they stripped the body of its valuables. As Dickens said in *Our Mutual Friend*…

Has a dead body any use for money? Is it possible for a dead man to have money? Can a corpse own it, want it, spend it, claim it, miss it?

5 The Victorian poor were known affectionately as 'The Great Unwashed'. Why? There was very little water in the poorer areas of town. What there was had to be taken from a standpipe in the street – when it was available. What little water they had was barely enough to cook with, so to save it they went without a wash!

6 The Victorian dead were more important than the living poor! When St Pancras Station was built, the railway company had to put a line through a graveyard. They had to contact the relatives of the dead and pay the costs of doing whatever the relatives wanted. But the homes of thousands of poor people were flattened – the railway company didn't have to pay them a penny!

7 Drainage was not introduced in London until 1865. Until then, water from sinks and makeshift toilets ran down old sewers into the Thames, or drained into huge cesspools under houses.

8   The Metropolitan Underground railway line opened in 1863 – steam trains pulled open trucks at first. In 1887, R. D. Blumenfeld wrote…

The compartment in which I sat was filled with passengers who were smoking pipes, as is the British habit, and as the smoke and sulphur filled the tunnel, all the windows haue to be closed. The atmosphere was a mixture of sulphur, coal dust and foul fumes from the oil lamp above; so that by the time we reached Moorgate Street I was near dead of asphyxiation and heat. I should think these Underground railways must soon be discontinued, for they are a menace to health.

9   A report on the Borough of Tynemouth revealed the following in 1851…

Eleven persons had been living in this house for a long time with no other means than thieving. They were feeding themselves with a piece of roast beef, eggs, tea and some hot whisky. The rooms of the house were in the most filthy condition that can be imagined; it beggars description. In one of the cupboards, having occasion to search there for some stolen property, there was a deposit of human filth; there were four beds in the room, three persons to a bed; behind the beds was a hen roost with a deposit of filth; the smell from the room was most overpowering. Connecting that room with the one above was a trapdoor by which a person could escape from one room to another when pursued by the police.

10 One of Victoria's least favourite towns was Newcastle. In 1850 she went there to open the new high level railway bridge. The London to Edinburgh rail link was now complete and she could travel from London to her summer holiday palace in Scotland without a break. She ought to have been pleased.

But, the story goes, a celebration banquet for the opening of the bridge was held in the Station Hotel in Newcastle. Before Victoria left, the manager of the hotel presented her with the bill for the banquet.

The Queen was furious! She vowed never to look upon the town again. For the next 50 years she drew the curtains on her railway carriage every time she passed through.

(But she allowed Newcastle 'Town' to become a 'City' in 1882.)

And even if you escaped to the fresh air of the Victorian countryside your life could still be very vile.

Vile Victorian work

Small clothing factories were known as sweatshops. To save money the workers were crammed into a small room, often a basement with no light or fresh air. To press the clothes that the women made, the tailor heated an iron on a gas or coke fire. The room was full of steam and the air was full of choking dust from the cloth. The wages in the 1890s could be as low as three shillings (15p) a week. Thomas Hood wrote this poem in 1843 about the girls who sewed shirts.

The Song of the Shirt

With fingers weary and worn
With eyelids heavy and red,
A woman sat in unwomanly rags
Plying her needle and thread –
Stitch! stitch! stitch!
In poverty, hunger and dirt.
Work-work-work
Till the brain begins to swim;
Work-work-work
Till the eyes are heavy and dim;
Till over the buttons I fall asleep
And sew them on in my dreams!
Oh men with sisters dear,
Oh men with mothers and wives,
It is not linen you're wearing out
But human creatures' lives
Stitch! Stitch! Stitch!
In poverty hunger and dirt,
Sewing at once with a double thread
A shroud as well as a shirt.

Thomas Hood

221

Vile Victorian factory work

True or false?

Rules for the factory workers were as bad as school rules. Which of the following facts were true for workers in Victorian factories?

1 There was to be no breathing between the hours of 9 a.m. and 5 p.m. True/False

2 There was a fine for whistling or singing while you work. True/False

3 Start work at 6 a.m. but no breakfast until 8 a.m. True/False

4 There was a rule against losing fingers in the machinery. True/False

5 There was a fine for talking with anyone outside your own line of work. True/False

6 Anyone dying at work would be sacked on the spot.
True/False

7 The managers would alter the clocks so you'd be late for work. Then they'd fine you for your lateness.
True/False

8 No young children to be brought by parents into the factory.
True/False

9 'Mould runners' – child workers in the Midland potteries – worked for 12 hours in temperatures of 100–120°F/I35–40°C.
True/False

10 Boy labourers worked for chainsmiths and used huge hammers. This gave them powerful, muscular bodies.
True/False

Answers:

1 False – not even the Victorians were that bad!

2 True – whistling or singing disturbed the other workers, the managers said.

3 True – 30 to 40 minutes were allowed for breakfast, one hour for lunch and 20 minutes for tea.

4 False – there was no actual rule against losing a finger, but it was one of the most common forms of accident. Less common, but still possible and even more vile, was the loss of a hand or arm; because of infection this could easily lead to death.

5 True – in some factories it was forbidden to talk to anyone at all!

6 False – but you wouldn't get much more than a minute's silence for your death; children had very little chance of getting payment for the death of a parent.

7 True – this was known to happen; there were once 95 workers locked out of a weaving mill; each one was fined three pence.

8 False – parents often took their children to help with their work; they were free labour for the factory owners.

9 True.

10 False – their frail bodies were twisted and crippled for life.

At least the Victorians improved life a little from the bad days of the early 1800s. The 1833 Factory Act cut the working day to 'only' ten hours if you were under 18 years old – and 'only' 48 hours a week if you were under 13. And the under-13s had to attend school, the law said. The trouble was there were usually no schools for them to attend!

The vile Victorian way of life and death

Life was hard and the death rate was very high. In Manchester, children and their parents were working 12 hour shifts in the factories and mills. If you were a child there was a good chance you wouldn't reach the age of 17, due to overwork, lack of food or the poisonous air which was all around you.

Accidents in the factories were common, but many died before they were old enough to work. In Manchester, in the 1830s, over half of the number of children who died were only five years old! An official report on the death of a woman living in one room with her husband and son, shows the suffering of those living in slums.

She lay dead beside her son upon a heap of feathers which were scattered over her naked body, there being neither sheet nor coverlet. The feathers stuck so fast over the whole body that the physician could not examine the body until it was cleansed. Even then he found it starved and scarred from bites of vermin. Part of the floor of the room was torn up and the hole used by the family as a privy (toilet).

Ten things you always wanted to know about a pauper's funeral:

The Victorians' obsession with death went so far that families would rather starve than miss one payment towards the cost of their burial. Those who died without burial club money would face the disgrace of ... a pauper's funeral!

Would you fancy one?

1 They were free.

2 You'd be buried in a public graveyard ... at the back somewhere, where you would never be found, as...

3 Paupers' graves didn't have headstones.

4 A headstone was 1p extra.

5 You wouldn't have a grave all to yourself.

6 You would share your grave with other dead paupers.

7 It was common for a pauper to share with more than 20 other bodies!

8 Burial grounds became so full with paupers' graves, that the bodies started to poke through the earth's surface, letting off a vile stench.

9 Grave diggers often had to jump up and down on the bodies in the mass graves, so that they could squeeze more bodies into them.

10 As for a religious funeral service ... there wasn't one.

Perhaps you'd hope a doctor could cure you before you died? Not if it was a vile Victorian doctor like Dr Meyers of Sheffield. He invented a wonderful cure for tapeworms in the stomach – a 'Tapeworm Trap'. It was a small metal cylinder tied to a piece of string. Some food was placed in the cylinder as 'bait'. To make the tapeworm hungry the patient had to starve himself for a few days. The trap was

then swallowed. The starving tapeworm would pop its head into the cylinder where it would be caught with a metal spring. The trap would then be hauled back up with the tapeworm - in theory.

Dr Meyers had to stop selling this brilliant invention. The tapeworms weren't killed … but the patients were!! They choked to death on the traps!

Weird Victorian superstitions

The Victorians claimed to be Christians but they had a lot of superstitions that were definitely un-Christian. Can you match each superstitious action with its consequence?

Warning – the following can be damaging to your health

1 Placing new shoes on the table
2 Rocking an empty cradle
3 Planting yellow flowers in the garden
4 Putting a garment on inside-out
5 Swallowing a spider in butter
6 Throwing the first Shrove Tuesday pancake to the hens
7 Drinking elderberry juice
8 Killing a spider
9 Turning your money over in your pocket while staring at a new moon
10 Planting a leek somewhere on the house (the porch-roof or a cranny)

OI! WATCH WHERE YOU'RE THROWING THOSE PANCAKES!

What will happen

a) Brings good luck
b) Will give you plenty of eggs for the rest of the year
c) Means the wearer will die within the year
d) Is a powerful charm against warts
e) Brings bad luck
f) Makes sure the family will be protected from witches
g) Prevents the house from catching fire
h) Will double your money
i) Is a cure for whooping cough
j) Means there is a baby on the way

Answers: 1 = c) 2 = j) 3 = f) 4 = a)
5 = i) 6 = b) 7 = d) 8 = e) 9 = h) 10 = g)

Most superstitious of all was the composer Schoenberg. He was born on 13 September 1874. He believed that he would die on the 13th of a month. Since the numbers 6 and 7 add up to 13, he believed that he would die at the age of 76. He died in 1951 on Friday 13 July. Of course, that made him 76!

Vile Victorian food

Vile Victorian eating habits

Frank Buckland, a naturalist, and his father, Dr William Buckland, had a taste for trying unusual food.

True or false?

The Bucklands ate…

Elephant trunk	True/False
Roast giraffe	True/False
A mole	True/False
Stewed bluebottles	True/False
Alligator	True/False
Mice on toast	True/False
Squirrel pie	True/False
Mice in batter	True/False
The mummified heart of Louis XIV	True/False
Roast ostrich	True/False

Did you know…?
The Sanitary Commission of 1855 found…

Vile Victorian food for you to try

Here are some recipes you might like to try. The Victorians ate them. They won't harm you and you may even like them!

CANDIED CARROTS

YOU WILL NEED
- 500g carrots
- 2 tablespoons golden syrup
- 2 tablespoons butter
- Chopped mint
- Salt

Now...
1. Use small carrots or larger carrots sliced length-wise Boil in salted water until tender.
2. Melt the syrup and butter together in a pan.
3. Add the carrots, cook for ten minutes, stirring regularly.
4. Serve sprinkled with chopped mint.
5. Serves four. Ideal with the Sunday roast lamb.

On the other hand, if you want to eat like a **poor** Victorian, then you might like to try this recipe from Mrs Beeton. She said it was...

seasonable at any time, especially during hard times, using whatever ingredients are available.

Half Pay Pudding

You will need

  250g suet
  125g breadcrumbs
  250g flour
  A handful of currants and raisins
  2 tablespoons treacle
  half pint of milk (minimum)

Now

1 Put the suet and flour in a mixing bowl and rub in thoroughly.
2 Add raisins and currants, and mix.
3 Slowly add the milk, stirring continuously until the mixture is thick and smooth.
4 Add treacle and stir well.
5 Place in a greased, oven-proof bowl and gently sprinkle breadcrumbs on the top.
6 Cook in a moderate oven until risen and breadcrumbs become toasted.
7 Serves all the family – but the more there are the less you get!

Vile Victorian facts

Test your teacher

1 Robert Peel (1788–1850) was famous for what?

a) Bringing the first oranges into the country – and that's where we get the phrase 'orange peel'

b) Founding the first police force – that's why they were called 'Peelers'

c) Being the first man to swim the English Channel blindfolded

2 Florence Nightingale was so ill when she got back from nursing in the Crimean War (1854–6) that she spent the rest of life in bed. But in 1890 she managed to…?

a) Have tea with the Queen

b) Take part in a charity fun run

c) Record her voice on Edison's new machine

3 William Schwenck Gilbert (1836–1911), the writer of the most popular Victorian comic operas, died at the age of 75. How did he die?

a) Drowning in his own pond trying to rescue a girl

b) On stage during a performance of his last opera

c) Choking on a chicken bone at a party to celebrate his latest success

234

4 Who wrote the dreadful lines of poetry, describing a pond:

> *I've measured it from side to side;*
> *'Tis three feet long and two feet wide?*

a) Famous Victorian poet, William Wordsworth (1770–1850)

b) Comic opera writer, W S Gilbert (1836–1911), in *The Pirates of Penzance*

c) Queen Victoria in her diaries

5 Victorians thought it was rude to use the word 'leg'. Instead they used the word:

a) Unmentionable – as in, 'We are having a lamb's unmentionable for Sunday lunch.'

b) Limb – as in, 'He's only pulling your limb, Jim.'

c) That-which-you-walk-on – as in, 'You put your right That-which-you-walk-on in, you put your left That-which-you-walk-on out, in out, in out, shake it all about.'

6 A Victorian husband had the legal right to do which of the following?

a) Lock up his wife

b) Beat his wife

c) Own all his wife's belongings, clothes and money

Answers:

1b) Created the police force in 1829. Fell off his horse and died 21 years later, probably while exceeding the speed limit.

2c) The recording was made at her home on a cylinder.

3a) He was teaching the girl to swim at the time!

4a) He also wrote the famous *Daffodils* poem. He wandered round the Lake District with his sister, Dorothy, writing poems. During the French war in 1797 they were suspected of being spies, making notes for the enemy!

5b) Some Victorians even covered the legs of tables and chairs so that ladies wouldn't be shocked by the sight of a naked leg! And instead of having to say the shocking word 'trousers', some ladies preferred to call them 'the southern necessity'.

6a) b) and **c):** **a)** until 1891, **b)** until 1879, **c)** until 1882.

MY POOR POOR HUSBAND TRIPPED OVER THE UNMENTIONABLE OF THE CHAIR, HURT HIS THAT-WHICH-YOU-WALK-ON, AND PUT A RIP IN HIS SOUTHERN NECESSITIES

Mad Victorian guide to travel

The richer Victorians were very keen on travel and exploration. They travelled the world to stop themselves from becoming bored at home. They massacred African wildlife to bring back lion-skin rugs, and they robbed poor countries of their historical treasures to fill our museums. Most travellers had servants to make life abroad as comfortable as life at home. But if you were brave enough to face foreign parts alone, there were guide books to help you.

Mad Victorian scientist, Francis Galton, published a book in 1855 called *The Art of Travel*. He suggested a cure if you felt unwell as you travelled in foreign countries.

Drop a little gunpowder into a glass of warm soapy water and drink it. It will tickle the throat, but clear the system.

Sir Francis had other good travel hints that you may like to copy. What solutions would you come up with for these problems?

1 How could you light your pipe while out riding in a strong wind?

2 How would you keep your clothes dry in a tropical storm?

3 How would you soothe blisters on your feet?

4 How would you stop your brain from overheating with hard work (like in a horrible history lesson!)?

5 How would you cure a wasp sting?

Answers:

1 Get your horse to lie down and then use it as a wind shield, of course.

2 Take them off and sit on them until the rain stops! (Why didn't you think of that, eh? Maybe Sir Francis wasn't so mad after all!)

3 Make a lather of soap bubbles to fill your socks then break a raw egg into each boot. (Okay – maybe he was a few fruit cakes short of a picnic after all.)

4 Have a hat with holes in to let the air circulate. (Sir Francis had one with shutters so he could open or close the holes whenever he needed to.)

5 Take the gunge from your pipe and rub it into the sting.

OOPS, IT'S GONE OUT AGAIN

MAD AS A HATTER

AND HE THINKS MY HAT LOOKS FUNNY

COR WHAT A STINK!

The Vile Victorian army

The vile Victorians set out to conquer the world. When they defeated another country they could take its wealth, and its natural resources (diamonds from South Africa, sugar from the West Indies, cotton from Egypt, tea from India and so on). The Victorians back in England could make even bigger fortunes by trading with the conquered countries.

To conquer these countries Victorian Britain needed an army. Queen Victoria was very proud of her army. The army was pretty proud of itself. And that's surprising, because they weren't very good.

Did you know – or, Foul facts about the Victorians at war

1 Flogging of soldiers, long abolished on the continent, continued in the British army till 1881.

2 The British commander during the Crimean war was Lord Raglan. He was already rather senile at the age of 67. He had fought against the French in the Napoleonic wars about 40 years before. He insisted on calling the enemy, 'The French'. The enemy were the Russians – the French were on Raglan's side in the Crimea. No wonder he lost his Light Brigade!

3 The vile Victorian poets didn't just write about love and nature. They enjoyed writing about war too. Adam Linsay Gordon (1833-1870) had all the talent of a five-year-old, but published this epic on war...

Flash! Flash! bang! bang! and we blazed away,
And the grey roof reddened and rang;
Flash! Flash! and I felt his bullet flay
The tip of my ear. Flash! bang!

4 The poets did have their uses in war, though. In 1857, during the Indian Mutiny, piles of books were used as a defence. Byron's *Complete Poems* was almost destroyed but at least it stopped a cannonball.

5 During the Second Boer War in South Africa, Queen Victoria ordered tins of chocolate to be sent to each of her 'dear, brave soldiers'. A bullet hit Private James Humphrey's tin and saved his life.

IT'S PRIVATE HUMPHEY'S IDEA SIR

6 The Second Boer War (1899-1902) was fought in South Africa against the Dutch settlers who thought the land was theirs. This time the British weren't fighting against natives with spears – they were fighting determined settlers armed with German guns. And they didn't do very well. The British wore red uniform jackets – this made them easy targets – but at least they didn't show the blood. One of Victoria's 'dear brave soldiers' was badly wounded in the face by a piece of shell. He had been lying for hours, wounded, on a hillside. At last he was rescued. His face was too badly torn for him to speak. He signalled for a piece of paper to write on. The nurses thought he was going to ask for something vital. But he slowly, painfully wrote just three words. 'Did we win?'

They nodded tearfully … nobody had the heart to tell him the British had lost!

DOES HE MEAN THE ARMY OR TOTTENHAM HOTSPUR?

7 The British lost many men in the First Boer War against a group of farmers and boys. At the Battle of Majuba Hill the British lost 93 soldiers. 133 were wounded and 58 captured. The Boer farmers lost just one person and five were wounded. One of the British dead was their leader, General Sir George Colley. Victoria sighed, 'Poor Sir George,' when she heard he'd been shot in the head … shot by a twelve-year-old boy!

8 Bobbie was a little mongrel dog and a tragic hero of the Afghan war. In 1880 his master was killed and the dog escaped to the British headquarters at Kandahar. His wounds were bandaged and he was taken back to England to be presented to Queen Victoria and receive his Afghan Medal from her. Having lived through the Afghan war it was a bit sad that he was shortly afterwards run over by a hansom cab and killed. He was stuffed and placed in a glass case (with his medal). He can be seen in the regiment's museum in Reading today.

9 The Indian Mutiny of 1857 was particularly vicious. As well as losing many lives in the mutiny, the Indians lost their nation's wealth. The British troops who captured Delhi began to loot it. One group stole a golden wine cup studded with diamonds. They decided to give it to their lieutenant. They reckoned he could sell it and use the money to but himself a promotion to captain. He sold it in London. It turned out to be one of the most valuable Indian treasures ever seen. The lieutenant sold it for £80,000 (or more than a million pounds today) and he became one of the richest men in England!

It wasn't only the vile Victorian army that got things wrong. In the American Civil War, General John Sedgwick looked over the top of his troops' defences at the battle of Spotsylvania in 1864. He scoffed at his men for hiding behind the defences. His last words were, 'They couldn't hit an elephant at this distan…!' Splatt! Bullseye!

The world's shortest war

But … the British Navy wasn't quite so bad. In 1896 the British Battle fleet was sent to Zanzibar. Said Khalid was trying to take over the country and the British wanted him out.

1   Rear Admiral Rawson told Said to get out of the palace by 9:00 a.m. Said refused.

2   At 9:02 fighting broke out.

3   By 9:40 it was all over. It was one of the shortest battles in the history of the world.

4   The only Zanzibar warship, an old British steamer called *The Glasgow*, was sunk with two shells.

5   The palace was destroyed.

6   But the British navy hadn't finished making the locals suffer. They sent a bill to the people of Zanzibar, asking them to pay for the shells used to wreck the place!

Fifteen foul things that Florence found – or, Flit on cheering angel

Florence Nightingale became a legend for her nursing work during the Crimean War in Russia. She visited Scutari hospital in 1854 and reported back the terrible conditions…

1 The men can lie in filth for two weeks before being seen by a doctor.

2 The men are lying on unwashed floors.

3 The floors are crawling with vermin and insects.

4 One visiting priest left, covered in lice.

5 Few men have blankets or pillows…

6 …they rest their heads on their boots and use overcoats for blankets.

7 Operations are carried out in the ward in full view of everyone.

8 The screams of the men having limbs cut off is terrible.

9 I had screens put around the operations – but they couldn't shut out the sound.

10 There are 1,000 men in one hospital, many with diarrhoea.

11 There are just 20 chamber pots between them.

12 The toilets overflow onto the floor.

13 Men without shoes or slippers must paddle through this.

14 Amputated limbs are dumped outside to be eaten by dogs.

15 Men are surviving the battles and being killed by the hospitals!

Did you know…?
Rearrange the letters of FLIT ON CHEERING ANGEL and you get FLORENCE NIGHTINGALE!

The vilest Victorian victory – or, I'm dying to attack those cannon!

The Victorian Army won a few battles – somehow! But their most famous battle was at Balaclava – that's right, it was so cold they had to invent knitted helmets to keep out the cold. Balaclava helmets. (To tell the truth there was another old knit in charge of the Light Brigade – Lord Cardigan! Honest!)

Anyway, Lord Lucan was in charge of the cavalry – soldiers on horses – when they fought the famous Charge of the Light Brigade. The Queen's poet, Lord Tennyson, even wrote a popular poem telling what heroes they were. But were they brave or were they batty? Make up your own mind…

The charge of the Light Brigade 1854

*'Forward the
Light Brigade'*

Was there a man dismayed?

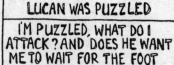

Someone had blundered.

Theirs not to make reply

Theirs not to reason why

Theirs but to do and die

Into the valley of Death

Rode the six hundred.

Cannon to right of them,
Cannon to left of them,
Cannon in front of them
Volleyed and thundered;

Stormed at with shot and shell
While horse and hero fell,
They that had fought so well
Came through the jaws
    of Death
Back from the mouth of hell,

Tennyson finished with the words…
When can their glory fade?
Oh, the wild charge they made!
All the world wondered.
Honour the charge they made,
Honour the Light Brigade,
Noble six hundred!

A Frenchman who watched the charge from high on a ridge had a different point of view. General Bosquet muttered the famous words…
It's magnificent, but it isn't war − it's stupidity!

Vile Victorian soldering – or, Let's have a whip round for the soldiers

Would you have liked to fight in the Victorian army? Smart red uniforms (made you a good target for the enemy!). Officers who lived like gentlemen and treated the men like servants.

RIGHT SMITH, AFTER YOU'VE POLISHED MY BOOTS, ATTACK THAT ARMY OVER THERE, AND IF YOU'RE NOT BACK IN TIME TO SERVE ME MY TEA I'LL HAVE YOU FLOGGED

And if the enemy didn't get you then your own army might! Apart from being killed by the enemy you could end up…

Flogged to death

Private Slim died after being punished by 50 lashes in 1867. He was lucky! In 1846 Private White died after receiving 150 lashes. In 1825 a soldier was sentenced to 1,900 lashes – they stopped after he'd received 1,200 and he survived. Maybe their arms got tired.

Frozen to death

At Balaclava in 1854 soldiers found something to help them survive the cold. Chocolate. But they didn't eat it!

Chocolate used to be sent out to us, this reaching us made up in shape like a big flat cheese; this chocolate we found would burn so, breaking it into pieces and piling stones around we would set fire to it, this being the only way we succeeded in staying warm for the first few months.

WHAT SHALL WE HAVE FOR SUPPER?

HOW ABOUT A CUP OF HOT CHOCOLATE?

Murdered

A sergeant had a soldier put in prison for gambling. He then had the man released … but the soldier wasn't going to forgive.

Loading his musket, he watched for the return of the sergeant and shot him through the back as he was about to enter his room.

Executed

Striking an officer could be punished by death.

One man struck the doctor while in hospital. He was shot. I saw this. It was early in the morning. Everything was so still that a pin might be heard to fall. The coffin was put on the ground. The man knelt upon his own coffin. The crack of the muskets was heard and the man fell dead.

Dying of thirst

Many soldiers died from lack of water in droughts in India. One sad case was of a soldier who helped to save the town of Lucknow. He received a deadly wound and lay dying. Some English ladies had been living in Lucknow at the time. The heat was terrible and the soldier was too ill to reach water. As the English ladies passed him, he begged the women to bring him a drop of water. They pointed to the well and said…

'THERE IS THE WELL, MY MAN, AND YOU CAN GET THE WATER YOURSELF'

He died.

Dying of Hunger

When the enemy cut off supplies (in a siege) the soldiers could starve to death. In the Boer War in South Africa, the soldiers managed to joke about their pitifully small meals. They said grace after a meal –

We thank the Lord for what we've had,
If it were more we should have been glad.
But as the times are rather bad,
We've got to be glad with what we've had.

And after all that…
If a soldier survived he retired.
The grateful Victorian government paid him a pension of less than 4p a day.

Vile Victorian villains

The Victorian villains were as vile as any you'd never wish to meet. The real villains would cut your throat, poison you, club you to death or shoot you just for the sake of your purse.

As if these thieves and murderers weren't bad enough in real life the Victorians made up even worse horrors in their books. Count Dracula, Frankenstein's Monster and Doctor Jekyll and Mr Hyde were all Victorian inventions.

The viler the crimes the viler the punishments. The Victorians liked nothing better than a good hanging to bring out the crowds. All in all it was a vile and violent time to live.

The real live vile Victorian villains

Jack The Ripper

For over a hundred years police, historians, writers and criminal experts have tried to work out who the dreaded 'Jack the Ripper' could have been. He was never caught. Why did he kill? Why did he stop?

Many books have been written by people who claim they can 'prove' who the killer is. But each new book proves the other writers are wrong. The writers have claimed that Jack the Ripper was the following:
Which one would you choose?

> A mad London doctor called Stanley
> A mad Russian doctor called Pedachenko
> An unnamed butcher
> A lawyer called Druitt
> Queen Victoria's grandson, the Duke of Clarence (Her Majesty always showed an unusual interest in the case!)

The Duke of Clarence's best friend, James Stephen (who was hit on the head by the sail of a windmill and became mad)

The Duke of Clarence's doctor, William Gull

An artist named Sickert

A bootmaker called Kaminsky

A believer in black magic called D'Onston.

Or would you go for one of the wilder ideas? Someone at some time has said it was…

A policeman (perhaps a senior policeman destroyed important evidence – to protect one of his officers?)

A man dressed as a woman

A cannibal

A Canadian wearing snow shoes

A woman – Jill the Ripper?

The truth is that nobody really knows who Jack the Ripper was. He (or she) killed just eight women but became a legend as the vilest Victorian of all.

If you ever find out the killer's true identity, and if you can prove it, you could sell your story for a million pounds.

Mary Ann Cotton

If the vilest criminal is the one who murders the most then Britain's worst killer of all time killed four times as many victims as Jack the Ripper. Men, women, children and little babies. And it isn't a man … it's a woman.

She lived in the North Eastern corner of England and not many people have heard of her. In July 1872, in West Auckland, County Durham, an inquest was held into the death of a little boy, Charles Edward Cotton. The jury had to listen to the evidence and decide how he died. Was it…

'Natural Causes' – he died of an illness?

'Murder' – did someone kill him deliberately? And how?

'Manslaughter' – did someone kill him accidentally?

'Suicide' – did Charles Edward kill himself?

Here is the evidence. What do you think the jury decided?

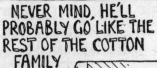

NEVER MIND, HE'LL PROBABLY GO LIKE THE REST OF THE COTTON FAMILY

YOU MEAN THIS HEALTHY LITTLE FELLOW IS GOING TO DIE?

YOU'LL SEE HE'LL NOT GROW UP

THEN ON FRIDAY SHE WAS STANDING IN HER DOORWAY AND SHE SAID TO ME...

THE BOY'S DEAD

DOCTOR KILBURN CAME AND EXAMINED THE BODY

CALL DOCTOR KILBURN!

I HAD BEEN TREATING THE BOY FOR AN UPSET STOMACH.. I GAVE HIM MORPHIA FOR THE PAIN AND HYDROCYANIC ACID FOR THE FEVER

255

ISN'T HYDROCYANIC ACID A POISON?

IT WAS A VERY WEAK MIXTURE YOUR HONOUR

AND WHEN YOU EXAMINED THE CONTENTS OF THE BOY'S STOMACH?

THERE WAS A WHITE POWDER THERE – THE STOMACH WAS INFLAMED

COULD THE WHITE POWDER HAVE BEEN POISON?

IT COULD – OR IT COULD HAVE BEEN THE MORPHINE I GAVE HIM

AND THE INFLAMMATION? POISON?

OR THE BOY'S ILLNESS. I HAVEN'T HAD TIME TO TEST IT

CALL MRS MARY ANN COTTON

I GAVE MY STEP-SON ARROWROOT – AND I BOUGHT THE ARROWROOT FROM RILEY THERE! HE HATES ME BECAUSE I WON'T GO OUT WITH HIM!

ASK HER ABOUT HER HUSBAND'S DEATH, AND HER OTHER THREE CHILDREN WHO DIED SINCE SHE ARRIVED HERE!

256

SILENCE IN COURT! THE JURY MUST FORGET THEY EVER HEARD THAT REMARK. NOW, JURY, YOU DECIDE. DID CHARLES EDWARD DIE OF POISONING? IF SO, WHO POISONED HIM AND WAS IT DELIBERATE OR ACCIDENTAL? OR DID CHARLES EDWARD DIE NATURALLY OF A STOMACH FEVER?

If you were the jury what would you have decided?

Verdict: The West Auckland jury decided that Charles Edward died naturally of a stomach fever! Mary Ann Cotton was free.

Then the local newspapers checked her past life and found she had moved around the North of England and lost three husbands, a lover, a friend, her mother and at least a dozen children! And they had all died of stomach fevers!

Doctor Kilburn then tested the white powder in Charles Edward's stomach. It was the deadly poison, arsenic. Mary Ann Cotton was tried for murder, found guilty and hanged at Durham Jail in 1873.

The vile Victorian children made up a nasty little skipping song about her. It was sung in the streets of Durham till quite recently. It went:

Mary Ann Cotton
She's dead and she's rotten
She lies in her bed
With her eyes wide open.
Sing, sing, oh what can I sing?
Mary Ann Cotton is tied up with string.
Where? Where? Up in the air
Selling black puddings a penny a pair.

Mary Ann Cotton got away with killing at least 15 and maybe as many as 20 people because…

1   Poison was easy to buy. Arsenic mixed with soap was sold in chemists' shops as a killer of bed-bugs. Wash away the soap and you would be left with pure arsenic.

2   Arsenic poisoning gave the victim sickness and diarrhoea – so did gastric (or stomach) fever. Busy doctors couldn't tell the difference.

3   A cheap baby food was flour mixed with water. Mothers fed this to babies and didn't realise that it gave their babies stomach upsets. Sickness in babies was very common. A doctor would see a sick baby and not think it unusual or suspicious.

4   Death was very common in the Victorian times. In the 1880s a quarter of all people died in their first year, a half were dead by the time they were 20 and three quarters were dead by 40. Mary Ann was thought to be 'unlucky' to lose so many during her stay in West Auckland, but nobody (except Riley) thought it was unbelievable.

5   Mary Ann Cotton moved about the North East. Each time she remarried she changed her name. Nobody could know the trail of deaths she left in her wake because nobody made the connection between Mrs Robson, Mrs Ward, Mrs Robinson and Mrs Cotton, who had all lost husbands and children in different towns.

Don't worry! Police experts reckon she would not get away with it today!

The vile Victorian make-believe villains

As if Jack the Ripper and Mary Ann Cotton weren't enough for the Victorians to read about in their newspapers, they wanted to read about violent crime in their books and magazines. Popular, cheap crime papers were called *Penny Dreadfuls*. New and horrific criminals were invented to satisfy the readers. Even today there are many people who believe these villains really existed. Villains like...

Sweeney Todd – the Demon Barber of Fleet Street

The sailor rubbed his bristling chin. He needed a shave. He looked along Fleet Street for the familiar sign of a barber's shop: a red-and-white striped pole. He soon spotted one over the door of number 186. The name plate said, *Sweeney Todd –Barber.*

The sailor pushed open the door and entered the dim and musty room that smelled of soap. A large, red-faced man watched him from the shadows. 'Good morning, sir! A nice close shave, perhaps?'

'Ah, yes!' the customer said and squinted through the gloom. The chair in the middle of the room was dark and heavy and hard. He sat in it wearily.

'I'll just bolt the door, sir,' the barber said. 'I'll polish you off then close for lunch.'

The sailor heard the heavy bolts slide into the door with a booming that rang through the room. 'There. We won't be disturbed!'

The barber picked up a bowl and a brush and whipped up a rich, thick lather. He began to talk while the sailor closed his eyes and lay back. 'Yes, nearly time for lunch. Have you had lunch yet? No? Ah, I'm the luckiest man in London, there. I live next to the best pie shop in the city. Mrs Lovatt's meat pies are famous. People come from miles to buy them.'

The sailor grunted and Sweeney Todd the barber brushed the foaming soap gently into his bristling beard.

'You've never heard of Mrs Lovatt's pies? You do surprise me! You must be a stranger? Yes? You don't know London then? No? And no one in London knows you, I suppose.'

The only sound in the room was the soft sizzle of the soap bubbles settling. The barber took a razor from the bench and slowly sharpened it on a leather strap that hung beside the mirror. He looked at his own face in the mirror and grinned. 'It's sad to be alone in a big city, sir. No one to talk to. And no one to miss you if you disappeared…'

Sweeney Todd walked towards the sailor with the razor catching a chink of light that had crept through the dust-crusted windows. He brought the razor closer to the customer's trusting face. 'We'll have you finished in no time, sir!' the barber chuckled.

Something in his voice made the sailor open his eyes. He looked up into the shiny face of the barber and the razor-bright eyes. He opened his mouth to cry out.

Sweeney Todd pressed a small metal catch with his foot and the chair rocked backwards. The floor opened and the

chair disappeared into a black hole. There was a cry of terror, a crunch as the sailor's head hit the stone cellar floor below. Then a sudden silence.

The barber put his razor down carefully. He pulled at a rope and the chair rose back into its place – empty now. A click of the catch and it was ready for the next customer … or victim.

Sweeney Todd wiped his sweating hands on his greasy apron and walked towards a door at the back of his shop. The door led to stone steps down into the cellar.

The Demon Barber of Fleet Street looked at the broken body of his latest prey and nodded happily. He crossed the floor of the cellar and came to the steps that led upwards into the shop next door. He tapped on the door and tugged it open a touch.

The warm smell of fresh-baked pies met his nostrils. 'Ah, Mrs Lovatt,' he said gently, 'One of your delicious meat pies, if you please.'

The smiling woman handed him a steaming plate and looked at him with one eyebrow raised, questioning.

Todd nodded. 'Yes, Mrs Lovatt. You'll find a nice, fresh supply of meat on the cellar floor...'

Of course, Sweeney Todd never really existed, but a hundred years later his story is still told and has even been made into a musical play!

Ask ten sensible adults about Sweeney Todd – or ten teachers if you can't find any sensible adults. See how many think it may be a true story. But it isn't! It really isn't!

The real dead vile Victorian villains

Public executions

If the real villains of Victorian Britain were caught then they faced fearsome punishments. They could be sent to the 'hulks' – ancient ships tied up by the river. By day the villains would break stones, clear sewers or move earth for building works. By night they would return in iron chains to the filthy, crowded ships where disease killed many. In 1841, at the start of Victoria's reign, there were 3,625 prisoners in these floating prisons on the Thames. By 1857 there were none. (The villains had been transported to Australia.)

WE'RE NOT GOING TO HANG YOU, YOU'RE BEING TRANSPORTED TO AUSTRALIA

IS THAT GOOD?

But they still faced the death penalty by hanging. And hanging in public.

Foul facts about public executions

In 1846 public executions were held outside Newgate Prison. Rich people paid between 20 and 50 guineas (a guinea was a bit more than a pound) to rent the houses opposite the prison to have a good view of seven pirates being executed. (That's several thousand pounds in today's values!)

Charles Dickens said…

I believe public execution to be a savage horror behind the time.

But he wasn't against executions going on inside the prison walls.

In 1856 a group of politicians from the House of Commons said that public executions should end. The House of Lords rejected the idea. They said that executing someone in public set an example to other people who thought about committing a crime.

The Lords' decision was popular with many people who did good business at executions … for example, the sellers of 'ballads' – popular poems written about the murderer. The poetry was usually awful.

Franz Muller was executed for the murder of an old man in a railway carriage in 1864 – the first ever railway murder. He tried to escape to America but was brought back to face a trial. He confessed to the murder in the final second before the gallows trapdoor opened and he fell to his death. The poems written about him were crimes against the art of poetry! They included terrible lines like…

> That fatal night I was determined
> Poor Thomas Briggs to rob and slay
> And in the fatal railway carriage,
> That night, I took his life away.
> His crimson gore did stain the carriage.
> I threw him from the train, alack!
> I, on the railway, left him bleeding.
> I robbed him of his watch and hat.

About 50,000 people attended Muller's execution. The day after, *The Times* newspaper reported…

None will ever believe the open manner in which garrotting and highway robbery were carried on.

In 1868, public hangings were stopped – not because they were inhuman, but because they caused so much crime and death among the crowds that went to see them!

The man they could not hang

Not everyone was as successfully executed as Franz Muller. Twenty years after Muller's crime, a middle-aged man, John Lee, had been working for a Miss Emma Keyse who had once been a maid to Queen Victoria. After an argument she cut his wages – in return he cut her throat.

He was tried and sentenced to hang. The hangman's name was Berry. Mr Berry placed a hood over Lee's head, put the rope round his neck, then pulled the lever to open the trapdoor. Nothing happened!

Berry jumped up and down on the trapdoor. Still nothing happened. Lee was taken back to his cell to wait while the machinery was tested. It worked perfectly. Lee was brought back.

Mr Berry placed a hood over Lee's head, put the rope round his neck then pulled the lever to open the trapdoor again. Nothing happened! Again Berry tested it. Again it worked perfectly.

Third time lucky perhaps? Mr Berry placed a hood over Lee's head once more, put the rope round his neck, then pulled the lever to open the trapdoor. Nothing happened!

It was thought that wet weather had swelled the wood and Lee's weight made the trapdoor jam shut.

The local justice ordered a postponement of the execution until the government minister had been informed of the strange events. At last the reply came...

Don't try again. John Lee is to be imprisoned for life instead.

John Lee's neck got away with murder!

Five further facts about John Lee:

1 Lee served 22 years in prison and then was released.

2 No one knows what happened to him after he was released.

3 Some people thought he was innocent of the crime. The sticking trapdoor was God's way of making sure that justice was done.

4 A film was made about the case and called, *The Man They Could Not Hang*.

5 A pop group has called itself, *The Men They Couldn't Hang*.

Criminals

Victorians thought they could tell a criminal by his looks and general appearance! Things they looked for were:

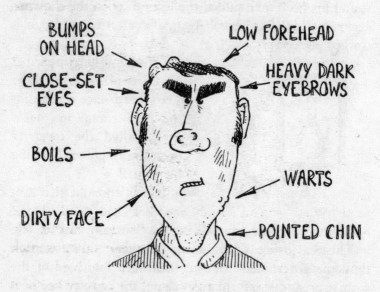

BUMPS ON HEAD

LOW FOREHEAD

CLOSE-SET EYES

HEAVY DARK EYEBROWS

BOILS

WARTS

DIRTY FACE

POINTED CHIN

...and anyone who was shifty or acted suspiciously. Most of the population were like this really!

The Victorian police – or, Has anything changed?

Sir Robert Peel had invented the police in London in 1829 to try and prevent the sort of crime the Victorians suffered. Perhaps they did some good but…

1 Early policemen were paid just one shilling (5p) a day. A shilling was called a 'bob' and policemen were called 'bobbies' (Bobby is also the nickname of someone called Robert – so they could have taken their name from Sir 'Robert' Peel).

2 Really clever people would be earning much more than a shilling at other jobs – so the police force didn't attract many really clever bobbies.

3 The police force employed practically anyone – even if the man could barely read or write.

4 The police force didn't much mind where a policeman

came from or who his friends were.

5 The first police only worked in London – within five miles of Charing Cross – and patrolled on horseback (not pandas)!

6 It wasn't until 1856 that the rest of the country had paid policemen.

Epilogue

The Victorian age wasn't all vile, of course.

The Victorians were energetic and inventive. By the time the old Queen died we had electric lights ... and electric chairs.

We had motor cars ... and crashes.

We had schools ... and teachers.

We had the very, very rich ... and the very, very poor.

Every silver lining has a cloud, as they say.

Charles Dickens wrote brilliant novels ... and he wrote some pretty vile stuff.

But, when he was writing well he was one of the best. He wrote a brilliant summary of France in the 1790s, after the French Revolution. He could have been writing about the Victorian age. It sums it all up pretty well.

It was the best of times, it was the worst of times,
it was the age of wisdom, it was the age of
foolishness, it was the season of Light, it was the
season of Darkness, it was the spring of hope, it
was the winter of despair, we had everything before
us, we had nothing before us, we were going direct
to Heaven, we were all going direct the other way.
A Tale of Two Cities

268

VILE VICTORIANS

GRISLY QUIZ

Now find out if you're a
vile Victorian expert!

HOWZAT VICTORIA?

The English lost a cricket match against Australia for the first time in 1880. They burned a bail to ashes and have played for those Ashes ever since. 'How's that?' the cricketers cried (or 'Howzat?' in cricket language) when they thought a batsman was out. And 'Howzat?' is the question about these curious Queen Victoria facts.

1. She was the shortest and the longest reigning monarch Britain ever had! Howzat?

2. Victoria was responsible for the death of her beloved husband, Albert. Howzat?

3. The police set Victoria up as the target for a murdering gunman. Howzat?

4. Victoria was highly respectable all her life yet she caused ascandal in her coffin. Howzat?

5. Albert and Victoria were married in 1840 though he never proposed to her. Howzat?

6. The Victorians liked portrait paintings but she preferred a particular kind. Howzat?

7. Victoria was Queen of England yet the 'Queen's English' was never very good. Howzat?

MANCHESTER MISERY

Not many men in Victorian England were gentlemen— which was unfortunate because gentlemen lived longer than working men. If you were an upper class person living in Manchester in 1842 youcould expect to live 38 years (on average). But, if you were in the working class what was the average you could expect to live?

a) 37 years **b)** 27 years **c)** 17 years

UMMS AND ERRS

The 1800s were the age of the melodrama. Before the days of television the century's soap operas took place in thrilling theatres where villainous Victorians battled against hapless heroes. You just know what they are going to say ... or do you?

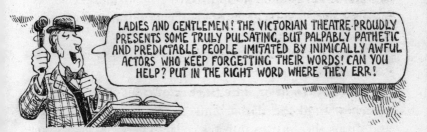

1. East Lynne

Poor Isabel leaves her husband but sneaks back (disguised as a governess) to nurse her sickly son. He dies in her arms as Isabel cries...

Oh, Willie, my child! Dead! Dead! Dead! And never called me errrr!

2. Youth

A bunch of English soldiers struggle against the enemy who must be evil because they aren't English. (The Victorians could be nasty racists.) Their colonel encourages them...

Remember, Great England is looking at you! Show how her sons can fight and errr!

3. The Fatal Marriage

Poor Isabella loses her husband and marries a dear friend. Then her first husband returns. She tries to murder him then decides to stab herself instead. (Don't try this at home.) Isabella sobs...

When I am dead, forgive me and errr me!

4. The Harp of Altenberg

Our heroine, Innogen, is captured by the villain, Brenno. As she tries to escape he grabs hold of her and Innogen cries...

Errrrme!

5. Sweeney Todd or, The Barber of Fleet Street

Sweeney Todd the Barber cuts the throats of customers and drops the corpses into his cellar. There his next-door neighbour collects the bodies and chops them up to make meat pies. As Sweeney cuts a throat he cries...

I errrrthem off!

6. Maria Marten or, Murder in the Red Barn

Based on a true 1827 murder. William Corder waits in the barn for sweet Maria but plans to shoot her. Corder sneers...

I now await my victim. Will she come? Yes, for women are foolish enough to do anything for the men they errrr!

QUICK QUESTIONS

1. How old were the youngest chimney sweeps in 1804? (Clue: not infants)

2. How was Lord Nelson's body brought home after his death at Trafalgar in 1805? (Clue: not a barrel of laughs)

3. John Bellingham blamed the government for ruining his business. How did he get his revenge in 1812? (Clue: a blow to the head)

4. Napoleon lost the Battle of Waterloo in 1815. What did Brit General Lord Raglan lose? (Clue: 'armless sort of chap)

5. In 1817 Brixton prison invented a new punishment for criminals. What? (Clue: hamster toy)

6. In 1818 Mary Shelley wrote a horrific story that is still popular today. What is it called? (Clue: frankly monstrous)

7. In 1820 in Scotland a rebel weaver was the last man to be sentenced to an ancient punishment. What? (Clue: long and drawn out)

8. In 1821 Queen Caroline died. What did this odd queen put on her head to keep cool while she was out riding? (Clue: American pie)

9. In 1822 King George IV visited Scotland and wore a kilt. How did he keep his knees warm? (Clue: they weren't loose)

10. In 1823 a boy at a public school, William Webb Ellis, cheated at football and invented a new game. What? (Clue: you have to hand it to him)

11. In Edinburgh in 1828 William Blake was accused of 16 murders. What did he do with the bodies? (Clue: they were a little cut up about it)

ANSWERS

Howzat Victoria?
1) She was the shortest in height but the longest in the time she spent on the throne.
2) The dirty water from her toilet leaked into Albert's drinking water and gave him the disease that killed him.
3) The gunman tried to shoot her as she drove in her carriage in London. His gun misfired and he escaped. The police told her to drive in the same place and at the same time the next day so that he could try again. He did! They caught him.
4) She was buried with a photograph of her 'friend', her Scottish servant. In her hand was a lock of his hair. What had they been up to when she was alive, people wanted to know!
5) Victoria proposed to him!
6) Victoria (and hubby Albert) preferred the people in the pictures to have no clothes on!
7) She was from the German Hanover family so she always spoke with a German accent.

Manchester Misery

c) In London slums people would, on average, live 22 years – but average upper class people would live twice as long. The unhealthiest place to live in 1842 was Liverpool,where the average age of death was just 15 years old. Queen Victoria lived to be 81. The average age was so low because lots of children died very young.

Umms and Errs

1) **Mother.** 'On the telephone' is definitely wrong! So is 'a taxi'.

2) **Die.** 'Fight and win' would not be very English – lookat the present-day cricket team.

3) **Pity.** 'Bury' makes a bit more sense, you have to admit.

4) **Unhand.** Not a word you'll hear very often but remember it next time a history teacher grabs you!

5) **Polish.** This is such a famous line your granny probably knows it. In fact she probably ate the pies!

6) **Love.** 'Get chocolates from' is not a good enough answer.

Quick Questions

1) Four years old. The sweeps weren't supposed to be under nine but employers lied about the ages of their workers.

2) Pickled in a barrel of brandy. It preserved the body – and the sailors drank the brandy afterwards!

3) He shot the Prime Minister, Spencer Perceval, dead. The only Brit PM to be assassinated. Bellingham was hanged.

4) His arm. He also almost lost his wedding ring when the arm was amputated. 'Here! Bring that arm back!' he cried from his hospital bed.

5) The 'treadmill'– a bit like a hamster wheel, where the prisoners walk and walk and go nowhere.

6) Frankenstein. Monstrous Mary was only 18 when she dreamed up this story of a man put together like a Lego kit. Seriously weird writer.

7) Wilson was sentenced to be hanged, drawn and quartered. In fact he was hanged then beheaded. His 'crime' was to lead a march in protest against unemployment.

8) A pumpkin. She probably changed it each time she rode, which is more than she did with her stockings. She wore them till they stank.

9) Tights. He had them made the colour of his flesh because he didn't want to look like a wimp.

10) Rugby. He picked up the ball and ran with it. The game was named after his public school, Rugby, so we don't say, 'Fancy a game ofEllis?'

11) He sold them to doctors so they could experiment on them. Of course the doctors weren't punished.

INTERESTING INDEX

Where will you find 'bottom-slapping',
'fried earwigs' and 'mice on toast' in an index?
In a Horrible Histories book, of course!

Afghan Wars 241
Albert, Prince (Queen Victoria's husband) 148-9, 152-55
American Civil War 202
amputations 245
army 239-51
arsenic (poison) 258
Ashes (cricket disaster) 149

baby-farmers 163-64
Balaclava, battle of 245, 250
Barnardo, Doctor (opened homes for orphans) 165-67
Bartholomew Fair 150
bears 200
bed-bugs 258
Beeton, Mrs (cook) 232
bishopophobia (fear of bishops) 156
black magic 253
Blackburn Rovers FC 201
bluebottles, stewed 230-31
Blumenfeld, R.D. (writer) 219
body-finders 217
Boer Wars 240-41, 251

books, serious 210-11
Boot, Mr (chemist) 148
bottom-slapping 200
boxing 198
brains, overheating 237
Brown, John (Victoria's manservant) 154, 160
Buckland, Frank (naturalist and son of William) 230
Buckland, William (doctor) 230
Burnley FC 201
Byron, George (poet) 240

caning 185, 187
cannibals 253
Cardigan, Lord (soldier in charge of the Light Brigade) 245, 248
cavalry (soldiers on horses) 245
cesspools 218
chimney sweeps 183
chocolate 240, 250
cholera 146, 150, 216
Christian, Prince (Victoria's son-in-law) 160
Clarence, Duke of (Victoria's grandson) 252-253
Cocking, Robert (balloonist) 150

Collins, Wilkie (novelist) 147
corn laws 214
Cotton, Mary Ann (murderer) 254-259
crime
    prevention 267
    punishment 184-187, 252, 263-264
Crimean War 149, 234, 239, 244

Darling, Grace (sea-rescuer) 147
death
    rates 225
    by flogging 249–51
    by hunger 251
    by ribbons 183
    in surgery 147
Dickens, Charles (novelist) 149, 188, 210, 217, 263, 268
disinfectants 147
Disraeli, Benjamin (prime minister) 154
doctors 163, 191, 227
dogs 196-97, 199
Dracula, Count (fictional villain) 252

earwigs, fried 231
Edward (duke of Kent) 152
Edward VII (king of England) 161
elephants 161, 230, 242

factories, rules 191, 221-25
famine 148
flogging (whipping) 239, 249
food, foul 230-33
Francis, John (gunman) 155
Frankenstein's Monster (fictional villain) 252
freezing to death 225, 250
French Revolution 268
funerals 226-227

gallows 264
Galton, Francis (scientist) 237-38
games, gruesome 194-203
garrotting 264
George III (king of England) 152
Gilbert, W.S. (composer) 234-235
Gladstone, William (prime minister) 154
glass eyes 160
Gordon, Adam L. (poet) 239
Graham, Harry (poet) 212
grave diggers 226
Great Exhibition 147
Greenwood, James (writer) 164
gunpowder, drinking 237

hags 158
hangings 164, 257
    crowds at 252
    public 263-64
    unsuccessful 265-66
highway robbery 264
Holmes, Sherlock (fictional detective) 148
Hood, Thomas (poet) 221
Humphrey, James (soldier) 240

Indian Mutiny 150, 240-42
industrial revolution 213
inspectors 193, 217

Jack the Ripper (murderer) 151, 252-54, 259
Jekyll, Dr/Hyde, Mr (fictional villain) 252

Khalid, Said (Zanzibar rebel) 243

laws
    child mine workers 147, 180
    corn 214
Lee, John (murderer) 265-66

leeches 161
lice 244
Light Brigade, Charge of 239, 245-48
Lister, Joseph (surgeon) 147
Lucan, Lord (cavalry commander) 245-48

Majuba Hill, battle of 241
Martineau, Harriet (writer) 157-58
Melbourne, Lord (doctor) 159
Meyers, Doctor (inventor of tapeworm "cure") 227
mice on toast 230
mines, children in 147, 172-80, 182
monkeys, as dinner guests 200
mould runners (child pottery workers) 223
Muller, Franz (murderer) 264

nails, hammered through ears 182
Napoleonic Wars 239
Night Soil Men (toilet contents collectors) 195
Nightingale, Florence (nurse) 149, 234, 244
Nolan, Captain (soldier) 247-48

The Old Curiosity Shop (Novel by Charles Dickens) 210-11
orphans 165

paupers 226-227
Peel, Robert (founder of police) 234, 267
Penny Black (stamp) 147
Penny Dreadfuls (crime newspapers) 259
Pilcher, Percy (hang-glider) 151
pillories 191
pirates 263
plays 206-09
Pratt, William W. (playwright) 206

Raglan, Lord (army commander) 239, 246-47

railways 218, 220
   murder on 264
   underground 219
rats 196-97
ratting (sport) 196-97
Rawson, Rear Admiral (naval commander) 243
Rothschild, Baron 200

Sanitary Commission 231
Schoenberg, Arnold (composer) 229
schools 149-50, 184-93, 268
seances 154
Sedgwick, John (American general) 242
servants, life of 165-72
sewers 197, 216-18, 263

Sheridan, Richard (playwright) 152
Simms, George (writer) 182
slums 225
snakes 200
soldiers, life of 249-51
speed limits 149
spiders, buttered 228
Spotsylvania, battle of 242
starvation 251
Stevenson, R.L. (novelist) 149
stocks 191
stomach upsets 258
superstitions, silly 228-229
sweatshops (clothing factories) 221

Talbot, William Henry Fox (photographer) 147
tapeworms 227
teachers 145-146, 152, 268
   screaming 191
   sensible 262
   terrible 184, 188-91
Tennyson, Alfred (poet laureate) 212, 245, 248

Thames, river
  prisons on 263
  sewage in 216-18
theatres 206
Todd, Sweeney (fictional barber/murderer)
259-62
toilets 147, 169-170, 195, 225, 244
Tottenham Hotspur FC 148, 241
trappers (child mine workers) 176

Unwashed, The Great 218

Victoria (queen of England) 147-48, 150, 152-61,
212, 216, 220, 235, 239-41, 252
villains 252-66

wages 167, 171, 175, 189, 214, 221, 265, 267
Walters, Margaret (baby-farmer) 163-64
wars 239-51
Webb, Matthew (swimmer) 151, 201
White, Private (soldier) 249
wigs 156
wildlife, massacred 237
William IV (king of England) 152
witches 229
Wordsworth, Dorothy (poet's sister) 236
Wordsworth, William (poet) 235
work 221-25
workhouses 254

zebra-drawn carriages 200
Zulus 151

Terry Deary was born at a very early age, so long ago he can't remember. But his mother, who was there at the time, says he was born in Sunderland, north-east England, in 1946 – so it's not true that he writes all *Horrible Histories* from memory. At school he was a horrible child only interested in playing football and giving teachers a hard time. His history lessons were so boring and so badly taught, that he learned to loathe the subject. *Horrible Histories* is his revenge.

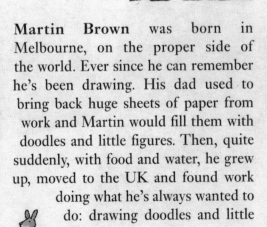

Martin Brown was born in Melbourne, on the proper side of the world. Ever since he can remember he's been drawing. His dad used to bring back huge sheets of paper from work and Martin would fill them with doodles and little figures. Then, quite suddenly, with food and water, he grew up, moved to the UK and found work doing what he's always wanted to do: drawing doodles and little figures.

ISBN 978 0439 94402 1

ISBN 978 0439 94400 7

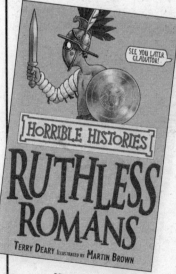

ISBN 978 1407 10424 9

ISBN 978 1407 10418 8

HORRIBLE HISTORIES

STORMIN' NORMANS

TERRY DEARY ILLUSTRATED BY MARTIN BROWN

ISBN 978 1407 10430 0

HORRIBLE HISTORIES

CUT-THROAT CELTS

TERRY DEARY ILLUSTRATED BY MARTIN BROWN

ISBN 978 1407 10426 3

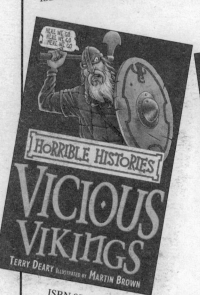

HORRIBLE HISTORIES

VICIOUS VIKINGS

TERRY DEARY ILLUSTRATED BY MARTIN BROWN

ISBN 978 0439 94406 9

HORRIBLE HISTORIES

MEASLY MIDDLE AGES

TERRY DEARY ILLUSTRATED BY MARTIN BROWN

ISBN 978 0439 94401 4

ISBN 978 1407 10425 6

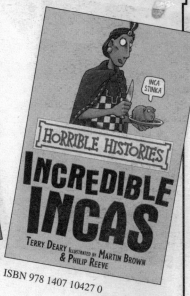

ISBN 978 1407 10427 0

ISBN 978 0439 94405 2

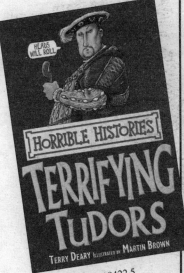

ISBN 978 1407 10422 5

ISBN 978 1407 10429 4

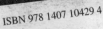

ISBN 978 0439 94404 5

ISBN 978 1407 10419 5

ISBN 978 1407 10431 7

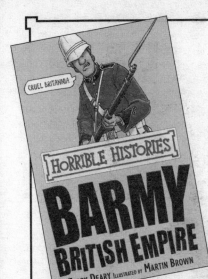

ISBN 978 1407 10421 8

ISBN 978 1407 10302 0

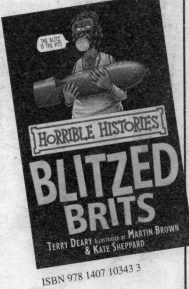

ISBN 978 0439 94399 4

ISBN 978 1407 10343 3

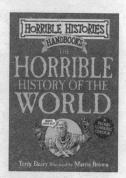
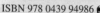
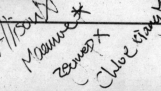